Practice Educating
Social Work Students

Practice Educating Social Work Students

Supporting Qualifying Students on their Placements

Wendy Showell Nicholas
Joanna Kerr

Mc Graw Hill Education Open University Press

Open University Press
McGraw-Hill Education
McGraw-Hill House
Shoppenhangers Road
Maidenhead
Berkshire
England
SL6 2QL

email: enquiries@openup.co.uk
world wide web: www.openup.co.uk

and Two Penn Plaza, New York, NY 10121-2289, USA

First published 2015

A catalogue record of this book is available from the British Library

ISBN-13: 978-0-335-26282-3
ISBN-10: 0-335-26282-1
eISBN: 978-0-335-26283-0

Library of Congress Cataloging-in-Publication Data
CIP data applied for

Typeset by Aptara, Inc.

Praise for this book

"When I read the book, I found it to be helpful and easy to negotiate, offering really practical and straightforward advice in an easy style. I would recommend it to all Practice Educators, whether long in the tooth or fresh in to the profession."

Steve Harding, Social Work Tutor, University of Leeds, UK

"An increase in expectations and practice standards, in recent years, now requires the Practice Educator role within social work to be enshrined in evidence-based educative practice theory, specialist professional standards, ethics and values. This publication consolidates professional practice standards alongside the PCF within the context of current social work education and would be an invaluable tool for practice educators new and old. It is clear, insightful and above all, comes from an experienced practitioner base. I wish I had had this type of publication when first starting out. I will have no hesitation in recommending this book to my own Trainee Practice Educators within and outside the social work field."

Kathryne Thomson, Associate Lecturer, Practice Educator Professional Standards 1 + 2 Mentor and Assessor, Practice Educator + Consultant affiliated to Bucks New University, UK

Contents

List of tables and figures

Tables

Figures

Abbreviations list

ADP	anti-discriminatory practice
AOP	anti-oppressive practice
APR	annual performance review
ASYE	assessed and supported year in employment
BASW	British Association of Social Workers
CAF	Common Assessment Framework
DBS	Disclosure and Barring Service
CPD	Continuing Professional Development
DDA	Disability Discrimination Act
DOLS	Deprivation of Liberty Safeguards
GSCC	General Social Care Council
HCPC	Health and Care Professionals Council
HEI	higher education institution
IRO	Independent Reviewing Officer
IT	information technology
LGBT	lesbian, gay, bisexual and transgender
NOPT	National Organization for Practice Teaching
NOS	National Occupational Standards
OSPE	off-site practice educator
PAP	Practice Assessment Panel
PAF	placement application form
PCF	Professional Capabilities Framework
PEF	Practice Educator Framework
PEP	Practice Educator Panel
PEPS	Practice Educator Professional Standards
PLA	Placement Learning Agreement
QAA	Quality Assurance Agency
QAPL	quality assurance in practice learning
SCR	serious case review
SOPs	Standards of Proficiency for Social Workers
TCSW	The College of Social Work
WBS	work-based supervisor

Preface

If you are reading this, you probably have an interest in supporting social work students on their practice placements. There is a wealth of written material examining the theoretical basis to practice education and learning. This is not one of those books. This is a practical guide, aimed at busy social workers and all health, education and social care staff who have volunteered to practice educate a social work student but find themselves wondering exactly what to do next.

Placements are rightly recognized as an essential part of preparing social work students for future practice. In tandem with this recognition, the role of the practice educator has grown in stature and importance, with clearly defined responsibilities and expectations. Gone are the days when it appeared acceptable for social work students to turn up, find themselves a desk and be handed the caseload of whatever practitioner was off sick, passing or failing based on little more than their ability to get through the duration of the placement without upsetting too many people. Thankfully, it is no longer acceptable for social workers to declare they left everything they learned at university at the door when they started work, and welcome the student to 'the real world', as happened to one of the authors on her first day of placement.

The current context of social work education

Wide-reaching reforms to social work education include the introduction of the Professional Capabilities Framework (PCF), to replace the National Occupational Standards (NOS) and key roles and the code of practice stipulated by the General Social Care Council (GSCC) are now defunct. The Practice Educator Professional Standards (PEPS) replace the Practice Educator Framework (PEF).

When starting out on your journey as a practice educator, it is important to begin with an understanding of the three main frameworks relating to the practice education of social work students. In the next section, we give an overview of the domain of each of the frameworks; please note that links to these frameworks have been provided in appendices at the back of the book.

The Professional Capability Framework:

- Sets out expectations of social workers abilities at every stage in their career.
- Provides a backdrop to both initial social work education and continuing professional development after qualification.
- Informs the design and implementation of the national career structure.

The Professional Capabilities Framework is split into nine domains (or areas) and each domain has different levels of capability to be achieved at different stages in a social worker's career. These domains include student-level capabilities, and it is against these that you will be assessing your student.

The Practice Educator Professional Standards are:

- Sets of standards introduced to standardize and outline the skills and abilities practice educators are now expected to have.
- Cross-referenced with the PCF at both social worker and professional social worker levels.
- Split into two stages with differing levels of responsibility for students set for each level.
- Outline the knowledge, skills, values and experience required to be qualified at stage 1 and 2.

Values

The PEPS document guidance links social work values to the assessment process. The values, as they apply to practice education, can be found in Appendix 1.

Health and Care Professions Council Standards of Proficiency for Social Workers

The Health and Care Professions Council (HCPC) hold the Standards of Proficiency for Social Workers (SOPs) in England. These are described as the threshold for proficiency below which registrants must not fall. The SOPs (HCPC 2010) have been mapped against the PCF domains for the level expected of social work students at the end of their last placement (that is, at qualifying level).

For clarity, this book will explicitly link to the Practice Educator Professional Standards, which we refer to throughout as PEPS. However, it is important to be mindful of the criteria set in the other professional capabilities frameworks.

These frameworks are perhaps a little daunting for those who are now being expected to contribute to the education and assessment of a new generation of social workers. Well, help is at hand.

The purpose of this book

This book was written with the express intention of guiding the practice educator or workplace supervisor through the placement, taking into account the PCF and PEPS requirements. It can be read in its entirety or dipped into as required. It could be the first port of call for those with little or no experience of practice education, or a reference and reminder for experienced practitioners. However it is used, it outlines the key information needed to adhere to best practice. It assists the reader in providing a high-quality placement experience, supporting their student to have learning opportunities which develop and test their skills under the PCF. It allows practice educators to develop their skills under the PEPS and is a quick reference, desktop or 'keep in your bag' guide.

Each chapter focuses on one specific element of supporting a student. Read together, these chapters will cover the placement process as a whole. Anti-discriminatory and anti-oppressive practices continue to be cornerstones of social work values and this should be reflected in practice education. For this reason, issues of anti-oppressive or anti-discriminatory practice will be integrated throughout the book.

What you will find in this book

As well as clear and sensible advice, examples and quick links to theory, and research, each chapter will have:

- An introductory set of key points, outlining what the chapter will cover.
- An overview of the PEPS that it supports.
- Good practice points, indicated by this feature in the text:

- A warning icon in the margin to remind the reader where they should be alert to avoiding common pitfalls, shown as:

Chapter 1 is a guide to setting up the placement and considers the purpose of the pre-placement visit, Placement Learning Agreement meeting and documentation. It outlines what needs to be done to prepare for your students arrival. It will help you get the placement off to a good start and goes on to help you to develop a good quality induction.

This chapter will also introduce some key people, examining their roles and looking at the contribution of the wider team in hosting the placement. The differences and challenges of setting up a placement as an off-site practice educator are explored.

Chapter 2 looks at enabling learning and development. We offer a brief overview of learning styles and consider adult learning. The role and importance of supervision is examined and ideas for establishing the students understanding of supervision are given.

Practical tools are suggested to enable you to identify suitable learning opportunities for your student, and we attempt to demystify reflective practice linking theory to practice in order to develop the student's social work skills.

Chapter 3 highlights the importance of fair and evidence-based assessment and the higher education institution (HEI) context in which it sits. It will help you to facilitate the student's self-assessment and includes a checklist of questions to utilize in reflective practice discussions in supervision. There is an emphasis on how to assess against HEI criteria. Some HEIs require a contribution to the marking of academic work. This chapter will offer advice should you be asked.

Seeking and utilizing service user feedback in relation to students' work continues to be a requirement and ensures service users' needs and views remains central to practice development. Suggestions for different ways of gaining and using service-user feedback are offered.

Chapter 4 looks at report writing. Guidance for writing the midway and final placement reports is given in this chapter. The circumstances in which a 'pass', 'fail' or 'refer' might be recommended, and the evidence to present in support of that recommendation, is examined here.

Ensuring the reports are fair, robust and fit for purpose is a given. There are also tips for including contributions from wider sources. The notion and justification of a 'constructive' pass, refer or fail is introduced.

Chapter 5 offers a brief overview of the wider course within which the placement sits, specifically how HEIs use quality assurance systems to monitor the quality of teaching, assessment and practice placements. It gives a straightforward guide to the practice educator's role in quality assurance responsibilities.

We emphasize a partnership approach to placements and assessment, and give guidance on how to be clear with students about when and how they are being assessed. The pitfalls of not working openly with students are highlighted.

Chapter 6 examines what happens if things go wrong. We consider how to manage problems that may arise on placement, and guidance is given on dealing with problems that originate with both the student and the placement.

We examine how to identify and address barriers to learning. This chapter also offers an account of the potential emotional impact on the practice educator if things start to go wrong.

Chapter 7 contains final thoughts to consider your own personal development and support needs. Professionals are increasingly expected to undertake continuing professional development (CPD) and this chapter offers advice for using both formal and informal support systems to that end.

Further resources and reading can be found at the back of the book.

Many social workers will tell you that their placements were the most valuable learning experiences of their courses. A committed and able practice educator can be the making of a great social worker. Conversely, poor experiences can damage a student's perception of and enthusiasm for the profession.

We are really proud to be social workers. We see excellent practice every day from other social workers and the health, education, legal and care professionals with whom we work. We understand the weight of responsibility all of those who are involved in practice education experience: a responsibility for their own best practice; to the student and the general public for maintaining high standards and the good reputation of social work; but most of all, the responsibility to the children, families and vulnerable adults with whom we work. However, with responsibility, comes reward and we hope you gain as much personal and professional reward from working as a practice educator as we do.

Reference

Health Care Professionals Council (HCPC) (2010) Standards of proficiency: Social workers in England, available at: http://www.hpc-uk.org/assets/documents/10003b08 standardsofproficiency-socialworkersinengland.pdf [accessed 8 Oct. 2014].

1 | Setting up the placement

In this chapter, we will outline:

- The importance of planning for the placement.
- How to involve the team in preparing for the students' arrival and the benefits of doing so.
- The importance of negotiating roles and responsibilities within the team.
- Getting the best from the informal meeting (or initial interview).
- The structure and purpose of the Placement Learning Agreement (PLA) meeting.
- Practical arrangements to consider.
- How to formulate an induction plan.
- The off-site practice educator and how they might be involved in induction.

Links to the Practice Educator Professional Standards (PEPS)

This chapter will help support your learning and practice under the PEPS domains and learning outcomes for stages 1 and 2 practice educators:

A 3, 4, 5, 6, 8
B 2, 6
C 1, 13

and additional outcomes for stage 2 practice educators:

B 10
D 1

Also 1.1 Values for practice educators and supervisors (see Appendix 1).

Background to social work placements

Many professions including nursing, childcare and teaching use work-based as well as classroom learning and it offers the student a valuable opportunity to test out theoretical knowledge in the world where they aspire to work once qualified. Professor Croisedale-Appleby comments (2014: 49): 'It is the quality of the placement and the supervision received that is most frequently cited both by students and recently qualified social workers as key in the initial formation of their own professional practice – it is that important.'

No doubt most readers will have experienced placements during their own training and will recollect these experiences with either great fondness or occasionally recall some quite miserable times. It is not vital that a student develops a positive affinity with their placement. Practitioners may not have enjoyed every placement but most will acknowledge that they still gained valuable learning. A placement may be set within the voluntary, private or statutory sectors and may also cut across services for adults, children and young people all with potential to offer pertinent learning opportunities.

Placement planning

Benjamin Franklin, in his famous quote, cautioned us 'by failing to prepare you are preparing to fail'. No amount of planning could guarantee that no problems will ever occur on placement, nor will it ensure that every student will pass their placement, but effective planning should help to minimize issues and can be paramount to providing a quality placement. While appreciating that time is a precious resource for all, particularly for those practice educators who have extensive caseloads, the planning of placements cannot be overlooked. Honest discussions in the practice educator's own supervision may help to identify how such a role can be realistically incorporated into their overall workload.

A student whose placement has not been adequately prepared for and who has not secured an effective induction will risk not gaining sufficient understanding of the aims and objectives of the setting. Such students may also not develop their confidence and struggle to fit in with the wider team. Ultimately, the lack of a comprehensive induction may put themselves, colleagues and even service users at risk.

A team approach

The practice educator has the overall responsibility for the preparation and facilitation of the student placement as well as for the ongoing arrangement of learning opportunities, support to the student and assessment of capability. Increasingly, the practice educator is also expected to contribute to the development of the workplace as a learning organization. Encouraging the wider team to participate in supporting placement may also fall to the practice educator. Unfortunately in some instances arrangements for hosting a student placement will be made without any prior team discussions. It may be that assumptions have been made that systems and resources are in place and that everyone within the team is prepared for supporting a placement.

We suggest that the whole team should contribute to the decision to offer a placement in the very first instance. This way potential barriers and practical issues can be explored and, in most instances, addressed. The benefits to a team of having a student are not always obvious and some of the positive aspects such as the chance for students to bring new ideas and the opportunity for workers to undertake their own development (by completing practice educator training) may need to be highlighted. In some instances team members may feel threatened by the prospect of having a student in the team. Such issues can be explored either through team meetings or through supervisions, and often such anxieties can be addressed through the sharing of information about expectations placed on individual workers and assuring them of their value.

Practical Tips: Preparing the team

- ☑ Raise the potential for offering the placement as an agenda item at the team meeting (clarify that hosting a placement is a whole team effort, listen to issues raised by wider team and ensure these are addressed fully).
- ☑ Share by email or handout a list of key points about the placement. For example, explain that the student will be allocated work through the practice educator and that the student will remain as a learner supernumerary to worker numbers, and explain the reasons why the student needs protected regular supervision.
- ☑ Ask for ideas for learning opportunities which can be offered to students.
- ☑ Encourage individual members of the team to volunteer their own expertise by offering shadowing and joint working opportunities.

The key roles in the placement

The success of a placement will depend on a number of factors, but the key roles that can influence the placement (beyond the student themselves) are the setting's practice educator or off-site practice educator and the HEI's personal tutor and work-based supervisor.

While all those involved with the host agency including service users and partner agencies will be encouraged to provide shadowing, joint working opportunities and valuable feedback in relation to the students' performance, it is the practice educator who remains responsible for the student's supervision, overall assessment and final recommendation.

If an agency wants to provide a placement opportunity but does not have a suitably qualified practice educator or does not feel that they have the capacity to provide the formal assessment and report writing, then an option might be for the placement to use an off-site practice educator (OSPE) who would fulfil these tasks. Such a worker might be employed in the wider agency and just come to placement to supervise and assess the student, or they might be an independent freelance worker who is contracted either by the agency or the HEI. The costs for securing an OSPE are taken from monies allocated to the whole placement payment. If an off-site practice educator is employed, a work-based supervisor must be appointed within the team to allocate work and provide day-to-day support and operational or case management supervision to the student.

When looking at those roles involved with supporting a student on placement we must remember to involve the HEI personal tutor and the placement coordinator who will be matching students to potential placements. This coordinator needs to be made aware of any serious changes that have or are about to take place in your team or wider agency that may impact on your ability to provide a good quality placement.

What do students need to demonstrate before they can be accepted onto a placement?

All students on social work degree courses are required to have passed a 'fitness to practice' assessment, which is completed by their HEI prior to the placement application form (PAF) being sent out. These assessments vary depending on the HEI but can include:

- satisfactory completion of observed interaction with service users
- assignments linked to values and a basic theoretical and legal underpinning of social work practice.

They also require:

- the completion of a satisfactory **disclosure and barring service (DBS)** check
- satisfactory Self-Declaration of Health and Occupational Health Screening
- evidence of understanding of the HCPC codes of practice.

The personal tutor will confirm that all of these tasks have been completed.

Once it has been agreed that the setting hosting the placement is able to offer a quality learning opportunity to a student or students, the HEI will make a match and forward to the agency the **placement application form (PAF)** prepared by the proposed student. Reading this application carefully can offer the placement agency a good first opportunity to assess whether they can meet the learning needs highlighted in the student's application. Any initial concerns should be discussed with the placement coordinator and the student's tutor. For example, the student may be seeking to secure opportunities to undertake group work but this may not be an intervention your agency uses. Such a conflict between the learning needs that the student identifies and what the setting can offer should be addressed at the outset. Frequently, opportunities can be found within the wider organization or with the placement's working partners. In some situations, appropriate learning opportunities cannot readily be secured and if these are critical to the student's development it might be decided that the placement would be unsuitable for this particular student.

The informal student meeting or initial interview

When the student arrives for the informal meeting it is usually the first direct encounter between the agency and the student. It can be a time of both excitement and anxiety for the student, as for some it may be their first experience of such a workplace. The PAF should be used to assist the practice educator to put forward questions about what the student expects from placement and also what the student might bring to the placement in terms of skills, experience and knowledge.

As a rule, students are informed by their HEIs that they are not permitted to 'pick and choose' their placement and are in the main expected to accept whatever has been identified for them al(though, it would be good practice for the HEI to listen to and seek to address any significant concerns). However, it is important to note that the placement itself does have the opportunity to decide against offering a student a placement. The initial interview is the ideal opportunity for a practice educator/placement to check out any niggling concerns. Resist underplaying the importance of this meeting by just having a cup of tea and a chat. Instead, prepare for this meeting, ensuring you use this opportunity to establish the student's motivation and previous learning experiences, and set out some general expectations of what a student on placement will be expected to do in your workplace as well as what you can offer.

In our experience, when things have gone wrong on placements, the practice educator has frequently reflected that they had concerns at the informal or learning agreement meeting but did not feel confident to further examine those concerns or act on them. Taking on a student is challenging, and if things go wrong, can also be enormously time-consuming. Get the preparation right and minimize the risk. Of course, you should not expect students to be operating at the standard of a qualified social worker. It is, however, appropriate for you to consider what type and level of learning needs you are best placed to support. The first meeting will be invaluable in informing you about the student's attitudes, interests and learning requirements. You can then select students appropriately from an informed perspective.

If for any reason, at this point, it is decided that the placement cannot go ahead, it is essential that you clearly explain the reasons to the student and the placement coordinator. If an OSPE model is being used and an informal initial meeting is being held by the work-based supervisor (WBS), it is advantageous but not always possible to request that the OSPE will be there (however, they might not have been allocated at this stage).

Pre-placement meeting or placement agreement meeting

The importance of this meeting cannot be over-emphasized. It is an opportunity for all involved to explore, negotiate and record important details, which will provide a framework to the entirety of the placement.

The meeting usually takes place before the placement starts. There can be occasions where this is not possible, perhaps for example if a placement has been allocated very late or where all parties cannot be present. In that instance, the meeting happens when the student has started placement.

We would strongly suggest this is avoided if possible and if it has to happen, it should not be any later than within the first two weeks. Preparation for placement is a strong indicator of its success and this meeting is a key aspect of preparation. The minutes from this meeting form the PLA and are a key tool for students and practice educators to negotiate a detailed understanding of what is expected on a practical and assessment level as well as identifying learning needs and opportunities. Leaving it until the student has started puts them and you at a disadvantage. For example, a student who has not been party to an agreement that half an hour is taken for lunch, may take an hour. Other team members are not aware, necessarily of exactly what has been explained to the student and may form an impression of a person who is lacking commitment and has a poor work ethic, through no fault of the student's.

Sometimes with pressures on everyone's time these meetings can become overly procedural and a 'tick box' exercise. However, time and effort invested in this meeting can underpin the quality of the placement and will provide clarity should problems develop during the placement. The arrangement for the meeting tends to follow the format in Figure 1.1.

Before the meeting

Consider what information you will need and prepare questions.

The task of typing up the notes from this meeting is often charged to the student but each HEI is different and the tutor will offer guidance on this. Make sure you know who will be responsible for this task before the meeting commences.

PLACEMENT LEARNING AGREEMENT

FINAL PLACEMENT – 100 DAYS

Start date of placement...............................anticipated end date...............

Days attending placement..

Reflective study time (please state where this will be undertaken)

....

....

Usual hours of working...

Has the student passed the assessment of readiness to practice (please give details)
....

Are there any times when it is known people will be away from the placement e.g. holiday, training?

Details of other staff that will support the students learning

In the event of the absence of the practice educator/practice supervisor the student should seek advice/support from:

Who will be responsible for line management of operational work by the student?

Learning needs

Individual learning needs of the student. Please refer explicitly to areas of learning identified in the final report at the end of first placement and any outstanding PCF areas.

Proposed work opportunities (please link to the PCF and the HCPC Guidance on Conduct & Ethics where possible):

Figure 1.1 A Template Placement Learning Agreement (*Continued*)

Are there any strengths or concerns that may affect the student's practice (e.g. academic work, attendance, punctuality, personal issues, health, issues arising from first placement)

Are there any reasonable adjustments required to meet the student's needs whilst on placement and if so how will these be met?

Induction arrangements; how long will the induction period be? What will the induction programme cover?

What key agency policies will the student need to read during their induction, (including Health & Safety Policies)?

Practicalities (e.g. parking, I.D., dress code, DBS check, does the student need to have any vaccinations such as the hepatitis vaccination? Whom should the student contact if they are ill?)

Resources available for the student (e.g. computer access, desk, phone etc.)

Travel whilst on placement (e.g. Is the student expected to travel during the course of the placement for work related visits? If so will the agency pay mileage/travel costs? What are the procedures for claiming travel expenses? Has the student got Business insurance for their car?

Clarification of roles (e.g. of practice educator, practice supervisor, personal and placement tutor)

Supervision (e.g. frequency, venue, responsibility for the agenda, recording)

Figure 1.1 (*Continued*)

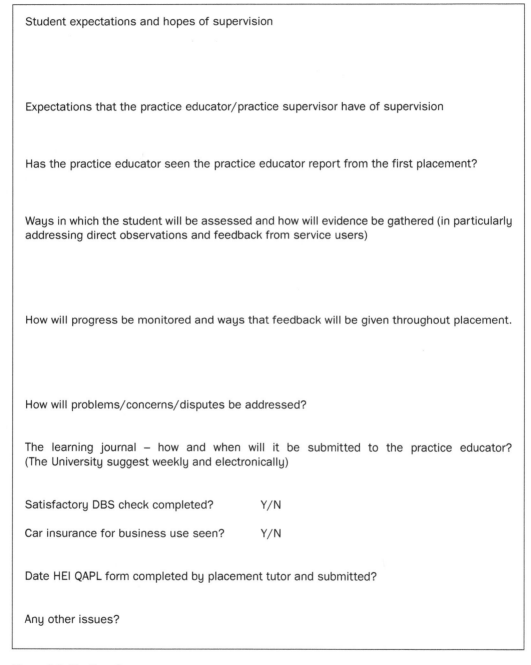

Student expectations and hopes of supervision

Expectations that the practice educator/practice supervisor have of supervision

Has the practice educator seen the practice educator report from the first placement?

Ways in which the student will be assessed and how will evidence be gathered (in particularly addressing direct observations and feedback from service users)

How will progress be monitored and ways that feedback will be given throughout placement.

How will problems/concerns/disputes be addressed?

The learning journal – how and when will it be submitted to the practice educator? (The University suggest weekly and electronically)

Satisfactory DBS check completed?   Y/N

Car insurance for business use seen?   Y/N

Date HEI QAPL form completed by placement tutor and submitted?

Any other issues?

Figure 1.1 (*Continued*)

<u>Dates of future meetings</u>

Mid placement meeting to be held on ....
The student and practice educator mid way evaluation report should be available for this meeting.

Anticipated hand in date for the student's portfolio (two weeks before end date): ....

The final placement review to be held on ....at ....

Signatures:

Student...date........................

Practice educator...date........................

Work-based supervisor...date........................

Tutor...date........................

Figure 1.1 *(Continued)*

It is the responsibility of the HEI that the student knows what is expected of them and they should arrive prepared.

They should also bring relevant documentation to the meeting. The placement should ask the student to ensure that they do bring these documents to the meeting then any potential problems with the documents can be identified and actions agreed prior to the student taking up placement, thus avoiding any delays in their start date.

The meeting

The meeting will usually cover **practical arrangements such as:**

- whether the student has an identity badge
- how travel expenses (if any) will be paid and who will pay
- how long will be taken for lunch
- start and finish times
- where and when the study time (if any) should be taken.

The meeting will also offer the opportunity to clarify learning outcomes, specifically:

- the roles of each party
- the aims and objectives of supervision

- the student can outline their learning needs (they should come prepared for this)
- the practice educator can explain the type of learning opportunities on offer.

The agreement may be amended at a later date with the consent of all parties.

Most HEIs require students to have completed and passed all outstanding academic assignments, linked to taught sessions prior to placement. There will be specific assignments allocated by the HEI for the student to complete while on placement, linked to their practice experiences. However, on some occasions a student might have outstanding assignments, which have extended deadlines or which need resubmission during placement dates. Such additional work should be openly discussed in the meeting as managing placement with such additional pressures can prove difficult for the student, and their lack of evidenced understanding of a particular topic may be detrimental to the success of the placement.

After the meeting

It is important to read the agreement and if you feel points have been missed or captured incorrectly you need to ensure that amendments are made, as an accurate record can prove vital as the placement progresses.

Case Example: Sally and Mark

Sally was Mark's first student and he was nervous about his first PLA meeting. Kim, the HEI tutor, had prepared the student before the meeting and Sally was aware that she would be taking minutes and had brought her DBS check, driving licence, car insurance and a copy of her previous final placement report. Kim had also emailed Mark the template of the PLA meeting and he was confident of the structure. He felt able to prioritize discussing Sally's self-assessed learning needs as well as encouraging her to raise any concerns or questions she may have. Sally was relieved at this as she had struggled to arrange childcare for her son in the mornings and she was able to negotiate a later start and finish to the working day. Mark reflected on his own placement experience as a student and recalled feeling abandoned by his practice educator who took a significant amount of leave during his induction, leaving him unsure of whom to turn to for support. Mark had been concerned that he was due to go on annual leave a few weeks into placement and was reassured as the meeting allowed for them to plan for his absence.

Afterwards, all parties checked the agreement for accuracy and signed the document. A few weeks into placement this agreement proved a useful record as it transpired that Sally had been missing lunch in order to leave half an hour early. Mark was able to refer back to the PLA document and remind Sally that a half hour lunch and a 5.30 p.m. finish had been agreed, explaining that this was a workplace requirement.

Anti-oppressive practice (AOP) and anti-discriminatory practice (ADP) in the context of the PLA meeting

As you will be assessing your student for the ability to practice in an anti-discriminatory and anti-oppressive manner, you must also ensure that you are practising in accordance with the same principles.

Clifford (1995) uses 'anti-oppressive':

> to indicate an explicit evaluative position that constructs social divisions (especially 'race', class, gender, disability, sexual orientation and age) as matters of broad social structure, at the same time as being personal and organizational issues. It looks at the use and abuse of power not only in relation to individual or organizational behavior, which may be overtly, covertly or indirectly racist, classist, sexist and so on, but also in relation to broader social structures for example, the health, educational, political and economic, media and cultural systems and their routine provision of services and rewards for powerful groups at local as well as national and international levels. These factors impinge on people's life stories in unique ways that have to be understood in their socio-historical complexity.

Gothard (2001) relates that to professional practice and is very clear that lack of oppressive practice will not suffice, one must be anti-oppressive:

> 'There is no middle ground; intervention either adds to oppression (or at least condones it) or goes some small way towards easing or breaking such oppression. In this respect, the political slogan, 'If you're not part of the solution, you must be part of the problem' is particularly accurate. An awareness of the sociopolitical context is necessary in order to prevent becoming (or remaining) part of the problem.' (Thompson, 1992: 169–70, cited in Gothard, 2001: 117)

In order to practise in an anti-oppressive way, there must be a conscious consideration on the part of the practitioner to be aware of and combat discrimination against individuals or groups. Thompson (2009) offers a useful model with which to do this. In his PCS model he identifies three domains:

Personal (P): This relates to individuals actions; for example, a person who calls their neighbour a homophobic name. The personal has to be seen in the context of the beliefs and values supported by the cultural and structural.

Cultural (C): This is about the commonalities or shared values within which we function. Thompson describes this as forming a census. For example, in the community around him, the vast majority of people denounce homosexuality and it is considered 'deviant'; jokes are made reinforcing this and people who object are denounced as overly politically correct.

Structural (S): Thompson describes this as the way in which the oppressive behaviour or views are 'sewn into the fabric of society'. Some institutions such as government, schools, media or religious establishments may reinforce this. For example, the media may portray homosexual people as sexually deviant and laws may withdraw rights from homosexual people, which are offered to heterosexual people.

To further assist with social workers' consideration of their practice, Dominelli (2002: 15) advises that there are three levels that should be considered when applying anti-oppressive practice:

1. Intellectual (understanding the methods and principles of anti-oppressive working).
2. Emotional (dealing confidently with oppression and discrimination).
3. Practical (implementing anti-oppressive principles in practice).

Consider the above as well as power dynamics in this first meeting and you have a good grounding for the rest of the placement. Naturally, you need to consider practicalities; is the building accessible, for instance? Also is the student a man in a predominantly female team, black in a predominantly white one? What might be the assumptions made by the team regarding the student's age? This last point is especially common. Younger students may feel they have to 'prove themselves' to older staff and clients who feel their youth is a disadvantage; equally, older students (especially work-based route students) may be expected to know how to get along in the organization with far less support and guidance than they actually need. The practice educator should consider such issues before the PLA meeting and ensure practical and physical arrangements do not disadvantage the student; for example, there may be a black workers' forum which the student can be made aware of and given the choice of attending, or a younger student who has no peers their own age could be paired for some shadowing opportunities with a skilled and young worker from a partner organization.

The 1995 and 2005 Disability Discrimination Acts (DDAs) require employers to make 'reasonable adjustments' to ensure that employees are enabled to undertake their work, and this extends to placement organizations being obliged to make reasonable adjustments to ensure students are given the opportunity to meet their learning outcomes. Despite this, many people will have experienced disadvantage and discrimination, and may be reluctant to disclose a disability. It is imperative that to the best of your ability, you support the student to do so and assure them it will be responded to appropriately and without bias. Ultimately, an organization cannot make reasonable adjustments if the student does not disclose the need for it to do so.

Higher education institutions have their own policies and procedures in relation to supporting pregnant students or new mothers. However the placement agency will also need to consider their own human resource policies and procedures and ensure that these are adhered to in such situations.

Practical arrangements before the placement starts

Once the PLA has been successfully conducted, you will need to spend some time dealing with the practical issues in readiness for the placement to commence.

Access to information technology

Most but not all placements will use information technology (IT) systems for case recording or communication purposes so if the placement team use computers then it follows that the student will need to access the same resources in order to comply with the agency's recording policies and develop and provide evidence of their recording skills. Although it can take some efforts to add the student as a temporary team member on to IT systems, it will be necessary and is maybe a task which can be addressed prior to the student taking up placement. If an organization has concerns about students' accessing such resources, then this is an issue which needs to be explored with the HEI prior to any agreement to offer a student a placement. We would suggest that limiting such access to IT would put the student at a disadvantage from their peers on other placements and limit their ability to evidence their skills.

Computers, as with other resources such as desks and office space, can be at a premium within teams, and workers often work a 'hot-desking' system. If this is the case, then of course the student should be expected to participate in the scheme alongside their colleagues. However, we have encountered situations where access to computers is limited and the student is asked to bring in their own laptop or tablet device to placement rather than rely on accessing equipment in the office. Where resources are in high demand this might appear a reasonable option but this is an arrangement that placements must carefully consider as it can be fraught with potential issues. Potential loss, damage (perhaps through corrupt data sticks or USB devices) or theft of the device are important considerations and making reparation to a student should one of these outcomes occur could cost your organization money.

However, the most important issue is that of service-user confidentiality and the ability to ensure the safety of personal and sensitive data. This is an extremely serious issue and your organization will almost certainly have a policy which your student should be made aware of. As a practice educator, you should follow dilligently any policy with reference to data protection and use of IT systems.

Setting expectations for day one

It is a good idea to write to or email the student before the start date to remind them of key points and to let them know you have not forgotten about them. There can sometimes be a few weeks between the PLA meeting and the start date. Below are some suggestions you might put in the email or letter.

Practical Tips: A welcome email pre-placement

The letter might include:

- ☑ Time to arrive
- ☑ How to access to building
- ☑ Where and when they should meet you
- ☑ Finish time
- ☑ Parking/public transport arrangements
- ☑ Lunch arrangements
- ☑ Dress code.

Induction plan

Induction periods aim to allow us to become familiar with the organization's work, polices/procedures and how our role fits alongside the roles of other colleagues both with the agency and with external agencies. Ford and Jones (1987) point out that for the student this is often perceived as a set period of time. On most placements, this induction time is commonly two weeks at the beginning of the placement. While we do take a practical approach to describing induction here, it is important to note that good induction is not only a set timescale and set of tasks, but a period of time within which the student can acquire basic knowledge and integrate with the organization. This necessitates you taking into account the student's previous experience (if any) of working in organizations as well as their individual learning needs when planning their induction.

What should the induction cover?

In practical terms though, we also do need to know where the toilet is and so on, so a tour of your facilities should be your first activity. Student social workers will need the same kind of induction as other team members to ensure that they are prepared to take on an effective role within the team. Utilizing the same induction plan as the agency uses for new workers might work well, although some adaptions may need to be made for students who may not all have had the same past work experience. Few people enjoy sitting at a desk just reading agency policies and procedures for days on end so please take a creative approach to the induction. A balance of shadowing experiences, orientation meetings with different team members alongside designated times for reading of policies and procedures can be more engaging and more productive for the student.

Another suggestion might be to offer the student an induction quiz based on elements of each key policy alongside questions about roles within the team. This can help the student read with purpose as well as offering the practice educator a clearer indication of whether or not the student has taken on board the information made available to them. Once developed, this quiz can be used as a resource for future students.

We recommend students are given an outline of the organizational structure, lists and positions of key people in the teams they will be working closely with and their status as part-time/full-time workers (with the days they work), plus contact details. This may seem obvious but, remember, much of the information you know about your organization has been built up over a long period of time and the student does not have this luxury. Students are expected to take some responsibility for seeking out their own learning opportunities. This can start in the induction. Practice educators can support this process by providing the student with a blank diary sheet with a list of suggested agencies and telephone numbers, the practice educator may fill in the first week, leaving a few slots for the student to complete as they see fit and the students can then be encouraged to approach colleagues from both the host and partner agencies and arrange shadowing opportunities for themselves for the second week. Students should be encouraged to discuss shadowing visits during supervision, and learning gained from such experiences can be explored. It is important students have a focus when shadowing other workers on their induction and can begin to identify and gather evidence right from the start of placement.

In summary, we have prepared the following checklist of things that your induction should cover, which you should tailor to your own setting.

Practical Tips: Suggestions list for preparing to host a student placement

☑ Access to a computer/laptop (sharing such equipment is fine if that is what the team usually do).

☑ Access agency logins to all programs used as part of the team's daily work (delays in securing these are common and can prove detrimental to the early part of placement).

☑ Make the student aware of routine office incidents such as fire drills (how and when they are conducted) and all pertinent health and safety issues in the workplace.

☑ Ensure key policies and procedures are accessible to the student as soon as they arrive on placement (this may particularly apply if they will have to wait for access codes to IT and the policies and procedures are online).

☑ Ensure there is an appropriate space to use, including desk and office chair (again, sharing of resources is fine).

☑ Do they have a phone and is it clear what their extension number is and how to dial out (if applicable)?

☑ Work mobile phone (only if required as part of students role, the student should not use their own mobile phone for work purposes).

☑ Access to stationery and other resources.

☑ Book time with an administration worker who can show them how to use the printer/photocopier etc. and run through any organizational practice such as room booking procedures.

☑ Access to any established lone working or buddy systems used by the team.

☑ Inclusion on signing in and out records or whiteboards.

☑ Access to agency updated policies and procedures (either paper or on line).

☑ Access to any agency mandatory training required by workers such as safeguarding or anti-discrimination training.

☑ Consider access to any pertinent support groups available to permanent members of staff such as worker counselling services, lesbian, gay, bisexual and transgender (LGBT) support groups.

☑ Provision of information to student about any changes, which have either recently taken place or will occur while the student is on placement; for example, changes to team structure.

☑ If work diaries are used, consider providing a diary to the student on understanding that as they exit they submit this to manager for any future reference.

☑ Parking arrangements if any.

☑ Identity badge or letter of introduction of agency headed notepaper.

☑ Day of team meeting and any other mandatory meetings.

The unwritten rules

In addition to the above we suggest some guidance is offered to the student about the 'unwritten rules' of the workplace. The 'unwritten rules' are not procedures or policies but practices based on subtleties of the organizational culture. These pieces of information can make a real difference to how well the student settles into the team and can help remove day-to-day anxieties which might otherwise prove a barrier to the student settling into the team environment. Unwritten rules might include:

1. The arrangements for tea and coffee funds.
2. Who buys milk and can workers just make a drink when they wish or are there set times?
3. Which refrigerator can they use? Is it acceptable to put packed lunches in there? Where can lunch be eaten?
4. Is there a washing-up rota and can anyone use any mug or does the student need to bring one of their own?
5. What are the rules about smoking?

The off-site practice educator model and planning

Throughout this chapter we have explored the various aspects of planning for a student placement but have not yet highlighted the differences and the challenges incurred in relation to placement planning when a model of an off-site practice educator (OSPE) is used. In most instances OSPEs will be approached either by the placement agency, who are responsible for paying them, but more commonly by the HEI who holds a list of off-site practice educators who meet their quality standards. Once the placement has been agreed their first introduction to the student, and possibly to the agency and tutor, will be at the PLA meeting. Although the timing is often not within the influence of the OSPE, we would urge those involved in such a model to seek contact with the student and agency at the earliest possible opportunity with the aim of taking an active role in the placement planning process. The PLA meeting provides a valuable opportunity for the OSPE to explore and negotiate how they will be involved with the induction process and to get involved in planning and induction arrangements. Before that meeting, the OSPE can prepare by researching the host agency, reading the students PAF and, if available, any previous placement reports.

2 Enabling learning and development

In this chapter, we will be covering the following:

- Use of self in practice education – how to get the best from students.
- An overview of and background to supervision.
- Models of supervision and how to develop a supervision contract.
- How to identify and arrange appropriate learning opportunities.
- Offering some suggestions for tools to be used in supervision.
- How to use supervision to develop reflective practice.
- Facilitating group supervision.
- Supervision as an OSPE.

Links to the Practice Educator Professional Standards (PEPS)

This chapter will help support your learning and practice under the PEPS domains and learning outcomes for stages 1 and 2 practice educators:

A 1, 2, 3, 4, 5, 6, 7, 8
B 1, 2, 3, 6, 7, 8, 9
C 1, 2, 5, 6, 7, 8, 9, 12

and additional outcomes for stage 2 practice educators:

B 10
D 1, 2, 6

Also 1.1 Values for practice educators and supervisors (see Appendix 1).

In practice education, as in social work, the use of self is a key tool in achieving outcomes. Behaviours on the part of the practice educator or work-based supervisor can significantly help or hinder students' learning.

Darling (1986) identified four types of 'toxic mentor':

Avoiders: Repeatedly and routinely unavailable. They will forget or cancel meetings at the last minute. They are not accessible on a day-to-day basis and if approached are busy with other things giving little time and attention to the student. This is usually the trait of a practice supervisor or practice educator who is not committed to the role.

Dumpers: Drop students 'in at the deep end' expecting the student to either sink or swim. They take little if any responsibility for organizing learning opportunities giving the student tasks with little guidance. A student is unlikely to go to this mentor for fear of feeling inadequate and may simply avoid the mentor and try to keep a low profile, attaching themselves instead to a more sympathetic mentor in the team. Dumpers are particularly dangerous as they leave service users at the mercy of unsupported and inexperienced student practitioners.

Blockers: Withhold information or resources from students, which would allow them to learn. They will not keep the student 'in the loop' with the team or alternatively will micro-manage students to the point of being oppressive and stifling any self-directed learning or ability to take risks.

Destroyers/criticizers: Only give negative feedback. They concentrate on faults and learning needs to the point of damaging the students' self-esteem while often inflating their own skills and abilities as experts.

In order to avoid being a toxic work-based supervisor/practice educator, consider your student's needs in the framework of Maslow's (1970) approach to motivation. He would argue a practice educator or work-based supervisor must respond to the student's needs as follows:

Physiological needs: In addition to ensuring practicalities such access to IT systems are in place for the student, the practice educator should take account or the student's wider physiological needs. Social work degrees are demanding and some students neglect their health, especially when lots of deadlines are accruing at the same time. The practice educator is within their remit if necessary, to suggest the student visit the HEI support services. For example, we have experienced a situation in which a student was struggling to afford her travel to and from placement as well as the clothing she required, so she was cutting down on meals. A referral to the student finance support office was helpful and she was able to secure extra funds.

Security and belonging needs: Students have to integrate into a team, which they will be with for a relatively short period of time. They may have little or no workplace experience and have the added pressure of academic learning and a constant demand for critical reflective practice. No wonder that they may feel concerned about being able to fit in! Practice educators can do much to help the student to feel a part of the team. A well-organized and thought-through induction will help, as covered in Chapter 1. Make a conscious effort to introduce the student to your colleagues and partner agencies throughout the placement; Ensure the student is included in team planning, meetings and any generic social activities. I recall one example of a team regularly going out for lunch and always leaving the student on duty in the office. This is not only obstructing the student's ability to feel a sense of belonging, but it is rude. The student's existing skills and experience should be recognized and explicitly noted. The student should have meaningful tasks, which contribute to the working of the wider team and organization. Ensure feedback is given regularly and positive feedback is given as well as areas for development. As a rule, we would not give feedback about the student's shortcomings or mistakes in public – but it is nice to point out in front of others what the student has done well.

Self-actualization: Though definitions vary, self-actualization could be seen as the achievement of a set of goals, which lead to a person fulfilling their potential. In the context of social work training – this is unlikely to happen on placement – whole careers work towards this. We are nothing if not ambitious for our students though, and supporting them to consider their social work aspirations in terms of abilities, skills, values, level of practice and so on is a really helpful activity and may form the basis of their ongoing personal and professional development, of which the placement and qualification processes are only the beginning.

So now we have examined the best use of self in our role as practice educator, we can go on to examine one of the main vehicles for developing our relationship with the student: supervision.

Background to student supervision

The importance of good quality, effective supervision has been the focus of much discussion in recent years. Such dialogues have been stimulated by findings from **serious case reviews (SCRs)** and prominent reports including those produced by Lord Laming (DCSF 2009) and Professor Eileen Munro (2011). These have highlighted that good quality, regular supervision is a vital tool in the promotion of good social work practice. Munro notes that experience gained from time spent in the social work setting needs to be unreservedly linked to time within supervision or case discussions in order to allow the practitioner to be supported to critically reflect upon their practice. Such an environment allows the practitioner to draw upon pertinent legislation, theory and research which can then continue to underpin their professional decision-making and ongoing interventions with service users. If we are, as a profession, to promote the learning from such SCRs and reports, then teaching our social work students to understand supervision and how to use it effectively feels like a very good place to start. When attained, such a skill will provide a valuable tool for the student throughout their entire social work career.

The basic concept of supervision is usually introduced through taught sessions within the HEI social work course but practice educators might find that supervision is still quite a new concept to students who may not have had any previous practical experience of the models of supervision used within the social work environment. As a practice educator

you will be expected to ensure that students secure a clear understanding of the purpose of supervision and of the roles assigned to the supervisee and supervisor.

Ford and Jones (1987: 63) offer the following definition of supervision of students on placement: 'planned regular periods of time that a student and supervisor spend together discussing the student's work in the placement and reviewing the learning progress'. To this we would add that supervision needs to be recorded and distinctive from what Ford and Jones (1987) describe as 'consultation' but which you may know as informal supervision. This usually relates to the process whereby the student is able to consult their practice educator/work-based supervisor on a day-to-day basis. It is usually in shared offices or where there is an open-door approach from the practice educator or practice

supervisor. While this process of the student being able to ask questions and 'run things by' their supervisor is helpful, it is not a replacement for formal supervision and will not be considered such should your practice be scrutinized if things went wrong.

Models of supervision

Supervision is in basic terms a process used as a tool to monitor, evaluate and develop both individual and team performance. An element of personal learning and development is needed in all supervision but it will form a substantial part of any student's supervision as they begin to link taught, HEI-based learning to their direct practice with service users. The benefits of effective supervision in social work are well documented but many of us will have had very mixed experiences when it comes to the quality and frequency of our own supervision. Providing supervision is a complex skill that needs to be developed, assessed and monitored to ensure that those supporting and assessing students are able to promote the student's safe practice and ongoing learning.

Requirements outlined by the Social Work Reform Board note that both level one and level two practice educators develop good supervisory skills, in fact, direct observation of supervisory skills forms part of practice educator accreditation. When exploring the model or style of supervision we offer to students it can be seen that, even within the social work setting, models vary across agencies and individual supervisors. Again when setting up placements HEIs outline specific requirements in relation to the frequency and basic standard agenda items they require as part of the supervision contract, and these tend to be included in the PLA document. The importance and clarity a supervision contract can offer is noted by Ford and Jones (1987). We would suggest that in addition to the placement agreement, practice educators develop a comprehensive supervision model and accompanying contract (some placement agencies already use such models and have standardized contracts which can be added to or adapted for the student role within placement). The students themselves may have some knowledge and experience of a particular supervision model or you may wish to ask them to research different models and work in partnership with them to negotiate a model and style of supervision which is mutually acceptable.

It is important to remember that the agreed model of supervision can be amended if either party feels that the format is not working (see Chapter 6). Kadushin (1992), Shardlow and Doel (1996), Ford and Jones (1987) and Brown and Bourne (1996), among others, have outlined three main functions of supervision:

Function 1 – Administrative or managerial

The operational aspect of supervision. It is concerned with the practicalities of the work and performance management, timekeeping, understanding of policy and procedure quality control and so on.

Function 2 – Supportive

The practice educator is able to support the student to manage the personal impact of the work. The student placement requires students to critically reflect on their own values and beliefs, and this may be unsettling. Alternatively, the student dealing with the impact of tragedy in service users lives will require support. Perhaps the support may be around occurrences in their private life and their impact on the students practice; for example, if a student is having relationship problems and is emotional at work as a consequence.

Function 3 – Educational

This might include supporting the student to make links between theory and practice, teach particular interventions which are used by your service, understand how the PCF and implementing social work values apply in the placement context and examining anti-oppressive practice.

Some theorists add the mediation role to this list and this relates to the role of the supervisor in engaging or integrating the student or worker with the organization. It may include explaining the role and assessment criteria to partner agencies too.

These areas, while they remain useful, have in recent years been criticized as being too compartmentalized and not acknowledging the importance of critical reflection of one's own and others' practice as a central function of development. Morrison and Wonnacott (2010) particularly criticized the emphasis on the administrative, saying: 'Supervision is not practice audit. The focus on performance management has come to dominate the process. Supervisors report that they are expected to use supervision to audit adherence to processes leaving little time to explore the quality of assessment decision-making and intervention.'

One way of checking if the student feels that supervisions are working for them is to include 'evaluation of the session' as a standard agenda item at the end of each supervision, which will offer both supervisee and supervisor the opportunity to evaluate effectiveness and propose any changes for future sessions. Once you have adopted a model of supervision, other items to consider for the contract might focus on issues such as role clarification, practical issues and areas of oppression and discrimination (see Practical Tips box below for further ideas).

Practical Tips: Supervision contract ideas

The contract could cover:

- ☑ Statement of roles for supervisee and supervisor.
- ☑ Outline of initial supervision model used (for example, Brown and Bourne 1996).
- ☑ Agreed standard agenda items (check placement handbook as HEI will have noted some agenda items which are expected to be covered at each session).
- ☑ Acknowledgement of power imbalance (ways that potential issues arising from such imbalance will be addressed).
- ☑ How potential issues/conflicts will be resolved.
- ☑ Practical arrangements (location of supervision room and room booking, responsibility for writing up supervision notes, length and frequency of supervision, and so on).

Such a contract is a working document, which can be referred to and altered with agreement of both supervisee and supervisor if changes to the supervisory process are felt needed. This document can also prove valuable should any issues occur later in placement (see Chapter 6).

Learning styles?

There are very many models of learning style and it is unlikely your student will have arrived on placement without having done at least one questionnaire relating to what type of learner they are. Among the most popular are Honey and Mumford (1982), who define four different types of learner and advocate the adaptation of teaching styles and learning opportunities to meet the particular requirements of each approach. These are outlined in the Table 2.1.

Table 2.1 Supporting different learning styles in practice

Learning style	Traits	Suggested methods for teaching/ learning opportunities in practice
Activists	Learn by doing. They will want to experience the work and are open to new experiences	• Practical experience: 'having a go' • Role play • Quizzes • Group problem solving exercises
Theorists	Want to understand the theory underpinning practice. They prefer models, research and facts	• Discussion of theory and research • Analysis of case examples and serious case reviews • Background information
Reflectors	Learn by observing and thinking about (reflecting on) what happened. They will usually be less eager to jump in and have a go, preferring to watch others in practice and discuss their thoughts about the intervention afterwards. They are able to consider a number of perspectives for any given problem and take time to decide on an appropriate action or intervention	• Reflective discussions • Self-assessment • Personality questionnaires • Observing others practice shadowing • Considering feedback of on their practice • Direct observations and reflecting on how they went • Learning journals
Pragmatists	Need to see how the learning applies to practice. They will experiment and try out new ways of working but only in so far as to find out 'what works' in practice	• Encourage them, in supervision to think about how they can apply learning to practice • Use of case studies • Problem solving tasks

The VAK (visual, auditory, kinaesthetic) model (Table 2.2) is popular in thinking about how an individual processes information about the world and therefore how information may best be presented to them to enable understanding.

Both of the above approaches state that learners may have more than one preference and they may differ in different situations.

Table 2.2 The visual/auditory/kinaesthetic learning styles

Preference	How this type of learner will learn
Visual	Through watching others, reading, having presentations shown to them on PowerPoint, reading charts or graphs
Auditory	Through being told, listening to audio recordings, listening to people's experiences, verbal feedback
Kinaesthetic	Learn by doing. They are tactile and will prefer a 'hands on' approach. They want to physically 'have a go' and often struggle to sit still for long periods. For example, teachers teaching kinaesthetic children tend to find that allowing them to play with some Blu-Tack while listening allows them to concentrate for longer

While popular, such theories are challenged by theorists such as Tennant (1997), who say that the claims made by learning styles advocates are overblown and unsubstantiated, and further criticizes them as they risk labelling and restricting individuals. There is little evidence to show that adapting teaching to a student's learning style(s) is effective. There is however, some evidence that teaching or presenting learning opportunities in a way which caters across the range of learning styles, does more effectively enable learning. For that reason, we recommend that when designing learning opportunities, you consider the range of ways in which students may learn or understand the world, and incorporate as many approaches as possible.

Theories of adult learning

It is now widely recognized that adults learn in a different way to children. This body of knowledge is referred to as **andragogy** or 'related to adult learning'. It is rooted in the work of humanist approaches to learning and outlines significant areas where adults' learning differs from that of children. Malcolm Knowles (1990) explains the differences as:

1. **Self-concept:** Adults are often able to take responsibility for their own learning; they are in the learning environment by choice and can participate in self-assessment. They need to be more involved in the planning and evaluation of their own learning.
2. **Experience:** An adult's prior experiences and learning are built upon in the acquisition of new learning. Thinking about past experiences and how they have impacted on the learner can be useful, for example via learning journals or reflective conversations in supervision.
3. **Readiness to learn:** The adult has usually decided they want to be in education and are willing participants in the learning process. They are therefore more likely to engage.
4. **Orientation to learning:** Adults are less likely than children to want to simply acquire facts about content and more likely to want to use learning to solve problems.
5. **Motivation to learn:** As a person matures the motivation to learn is internal.

While there are certainly exceptions to these 'rules', they are a useful guide to think about in relation to how you approach setting up a placement which facilitates adult learning.

Learning opportunities

Social work takes place across a broad spectrum of settings and these settings are managed across statutory, voluntary and private sector providers. What these settings all have in common is the ability to provide some excellent learning opportunities for social work students.

While it is a usual practice for HEIs to use placement providers who themselves employ social workers, there are high-quality and innovative placements in which this is not the case and where the practice educator is arranged from outside the provider organization, with the host providing a work-based supervisor on site (Croisedale-Appleby 2014).

You will have responsibility for ensuring students secure the relevant learning opportunities to meet the Professional Capabilities Framework (PCF). Learning opportunities can prove a bone of contention as the type of opportunity open to students will of course vary in presentation across the broad spectrum of placements, and students can feel anxious when comparing experiences with their peers. It is the practice educator's role to steer students away from the trap of feeling that only case conferences, court appearances and complex statutory assessments will provide them with the opportunity to demonstrate their skills and knowledge base.

There are occasions when both practice educators and students feel that a specific learning need(s) cannot be addressed by the work undertaken by the host placement. On these occasions we need to be proactive in negotiating and securing wider learning opportunities for the student. Again, in the spirit of developing the student's ability to identify their own learning opportunities, it may be appropriate to support them to look for potential partnership arrangements where they can extend their learning opportunities (bringing them to supervision to discuss before approaching the other agency). A first port of call might be to look at the wider agency to check if learning opportunities can be secured with other departments. Other learning opportunities might also be arranged with the host agency's partners.

Below are some case examples for further reflection, showing a good and a poor example of how students can secure learning opportunities.

Case Example: A student securing other learning opportunities well

Student: I'm really concerned that I'm just not going to be able to meet all the domains . . .

Practice educator: Let's look through where we have agreed you have learning needs (refers to PLA with students learning needs as well as template for midway report and the domains). Talk me through where you feel you have gaps.

Student: Well, here . . . I can stretch it and say that I have knowledge of the legal framework but I don't feel confident and the organization doesn't deal directly with any of the legal frameworks which impact on elderly people. I have had lots of experience of the initial assessments though and I get a lot out of the group work.

Practice educator: I have looked through your supervision notes and we have discussed the impact of housing law on some of the service users but you are right, that was quite theoretical. What do you think you are missing?

Student: I would just like to know I can respond to a service user in practice and feel confident that I am working within the legal framework appropriate to them.

Practice educator: Have you identified other agencies, which also work with our service users where you think you may gain this experience?

Student: Well, the hospital social work team where we get a few of our referrals from, they were talking about a safeguarding referral for Margaret, and Deprivation of Liberty Safeguards (DOLS).

Practice educator: I would be happy to have you spend some agreed periods of time with them if they are able to offer you the opportunity.

Student: Shall I ask the manager when I see him on Tuesday?

Practice educator: I think that is a really good idea. Remember to explain I have agreed it and outline what you want to learn about. I think we need to consider the time you can be with them, I would suggest a half day each week until the piece of work is done but come back to me if you need to discuss that.

Case Example: A student's poor attempt at securing other learning opportunities

Student: I wish I wasn't on this placement. All the other students at university are doing real social work on theirs and I'm not going to be able to meet the requirements!

Practice educator: Let's look through where we have agreed you have learning needs (refers to notes of students learning needs as well as template for midway report out and the domains). Talk me through where you feel you have gaps.

Student: Well I can't really see that I'm doing much real social work, I haven't done any law at all and I think I'd be better in the hospital social work team next door. They have a student and he says he is meeting all of his needs. I've asked him and he says I can just spend my time with him because his placement supervisor's really nice and he doesn't mind me tagging along.

Practice educator: I think it's really important that we look at the specific learning needs you have and where you feel there are still gaps. You are on placement here, not at the hospital. There are learning opportunities such as doing the initial assessment, which you haven't showed much enthusiasm for. Also in our last supervision notes, you still hadn't done the planning for the group work we were going to organize with the group of older people with Alzheimer's. This would provide some opportunity to meet your learning needs in managing your time and workload effectively, and applying social work theory, as well as reflective practice if we did a good evaluation after each session, all of which we identified as learning needs. I wonder what is stopping you doing that and why you feel so strongly that the only answer to your problems is to go to another setting?

Student: I just think I am a master's student and the university should have given me a . . . well a stronger placement really, if I'm honest . . .

Practice educator: I'm pleased you do feel you can be honest! I think we might be making progress. I want you to have a good placement experience and sometimes we have to challenge students to stretch them. I'm going to challenge you now and suggest you are perhaps struggling to 'recognize the role of the professional social worker in a range of contexts', you can see here, that's an important part of domain 1, professionalism, in the PCF. I am happy to look at how we can work together to ensure you are getting every opportunity to meet your learning needs but part of that needs to be you being able to recognize them when they are there. I would like it if you used your feelings about the placement as the subject for your next learning journal and reflected on what values and assumptions you might be bringing to the situation as well as why you haven't taken up some of the opportunities offered to you. Can you do that?

Student: Well, OK, but I still want to look at spending time at the hospital.

Practice educator: I think when you have sent me this learning journal and perhaps a list of the requirements you feel you are not able to meet here, we will discuss them. If I agree with your assessment, I will be more than happy to look at options for working with a partner agency that can best offer you the opportunities this placement lacks. If that does happen though, we need to be clear that it will be for a limited period of time, for example half a day a week for six weeks depending on the piece of work and that your main placement is in this project. How does that sound?

Have you had experiences with good or bad student responses like these as a practice educator? Reflect on the way the practice educator handled the two very different students, and consider how you might have addressed each situation.

Opportunities in other settings are one way but as practice educator you can also offer exercises and tasks set in supervision that are devised to address specific unmet learning outcomes. These exercises can complement practical experiences gained by the student during shadowing or observational visits and can provide measurable evidence of the student's understanding or otherwise of issues. Practice educator colleagues are a good source of knowledge when it comes to effective tools to use in supervision or students study time and like keen gardeners, they are usually enthusiastic about sharing their knowledge and resources. Resources frequently used include case studies, exercises based on SCR findings or exercises that explore professional boundaries. With practice, you may become confident at developing some of your own tools to use in supervision and we would encourage you to develop such resources, which apply specifically to your placement agency's work.

Learning opportunities should be regularly explored and evaluated during supervision and part of the role of the practice educator is to support the student to begin to recognize and arrange some for themselves. Table 2.3 offers some examples of just a few of the learning opportunities that might be taken up by a student.

All learning opportunities and the student's evidenced capability must be clearly recorded as the placement progresses. This can then be used as evidence for the midway and final reviews.

Supervisory tools

We need to ensure from the outset that we secure a mutual understanding of the aims and objective of the supervisory process.

To use an example to highlight common pitfalls in supervision, during an initial supervision session with a new student on her first placement the student shared that she had felt quite high levels of anxiety prior to the supervision meeting. When questioned why this had provoked such anxiety, the student said she had no idea of what supervision actually was having no previous experience. The student's only frame of reference for supervision had been her father's comments about his own experience of supervision in car sales, where the process was used by his manager to purely reprimand or dismiss workers for poor levels of productivity.

Any such confusion about the purpose and process of supervision can be alleviated at an early stage by requiring all students to do some basic preparation work. A good place to start can be to ask the student to undertake some reading around social work supervision and also ask them to note down a few responses to the exercise below (this can be emailed before the first supervision session).

Pre- supervision exercise

- What, if any past experience of supervision have you had?
- Why do you think social workers need to have supervision?
- What if any would be your greatest concern about supervision whilst on placement?
- What are your expectations or hopes of supervision while on placement?

Table 2.3 Learning opportunities at first and second placements

PCF DOMAINS (selected examples)	Suggested learning opportunity to develop capability for end of first placement	Suggested learning opportunity to develop capability for end of second placement
Critical reflection and analysis (domain 6)	Student can submit learning journals reflecting on case examples they have co-worked or shadowed on placement and discuss them in supervision. With support and guidance, they show an increased ability to reflect on their own practice, analyse the situations and use the learning from this to plan for their next contact	Student can be the lead case holder, for example in a **common assessment framework (CAF)** and can bring their analysis of cases to supervision, justifying their proposed interventions to their supervisor and responding appropriately to challenge. Once agreed, the student can explain the proposed intervention and the reasons for it to service users and professionals as required and conduct or coordinate the intervention
Diversity (domain 3)	The student can discuss in supervision or in their reflective journals where they have identified potential oppression and discrimination faced by the service user group or individual they are working with on placement and discuss how this oppression and or discrimination might impact on the service user	The student can demonstrate through either supervision case discussion or through their reflective journals how they have identified and challenged/ considered their own values and beliefs or actions in relation to the potential for oppressive or discriminatory practice with a service user. They can evidence what they have done, for example, secure a translator for some health promotion leaflets. The student can say how they will use the experience to inform future practice
Knowledge (domain 5)	Student shows an increased ability to identify the current legislation and local policy which applies to individuals or groups whom they are working with and can discuss these in relation to a case study or in supervision discussions	Student is able to identify and understand how legislation and local policy impacts on the service user, the placement agency's responsibility and on their own role/duty. The student shows how they have incorporated this knowledge into their own assessments and planning

Common
!
Pitfalls

As mentioned above, there is a need to acknowledge and explore with students issues of power difference between yourself as practice educator and them as a student learner.

This is not always an easy subject to discuss and you may wish to use simple exercises during early supervision sessions to aid this task. For example, in most final reports, practice educators and students are asked to submit a short pen portrait which outlines some background information about themselves. While this task is often left to the end of placement, the exchange of such information at the beginning of placement can be helpfully used in early supervision. Both the student and practice educator can identify areas where they are different and areas where they may have similarities. These differences and similarities can then be further explored with particular reference to any power imbalances (for example, gender or age) or barriers to learning.

Howe and Gray (2013), suggest that power in the context of student and practice educator is both formal and informal:

- **Formal power:** is the power that is invested by virtue of doing the role of practice educating. The practice educator has power because they are ultimately responsible for the assessment of the student's capability and therefore whether they will successfully pass the placement.
- **Informal power:** relates to the practice educators skills as a social worker and how they are used in the supervisory relationship as well as their personal attributes and approach. Informal power is also a result of structurally determined factors such as gender, race, class, (dis)ability and so on which if not explored may impact negatively on the student/practice educator relationship.

Using supervision to demystify reflection

A key function of the supervisory role for a practice educator is to support the student to secure and develop their basic skills in reflective practice and critical thinking.

Reflective practice can be thought of as learning through and from experience in order to gain new insights into one's own practice. It requires the practitioner to examine their own assumptions and to be self-aware and able to critically evaluate their practice (Finlay 2008).

In relation to reflective practice, Fook and Gardner (2007) say that our 'ways of teaching and learning need to be scrutinized for their capacity to foster ability to learn from practice experience, to formulate contextual knowledge, to be open to differences and to reaffirm the broader values and missions of the social work profession'. This ties in with the notion of reflexivity, as involving reflecting not only on the practitioner's actions but also on the wider social and professional culture within which they are operating (Taylor and White 2000).

Critical thinking is defined by Kurfiss (1989: 42) as: 'The process of figuring out what to believe or not about a situation, phenomenon, problem or controversy for which no single definitive answer or solution exists. The term implies a diligent, open-minded search for understanding rather than for discovery of a necessary conclusion.'

Students come to placement having completed taught sessions and assignments, which will have provided them with an overview of reflective practice and critical thinking. However, the transference of the reflective process to the placement setting can be daunting for students, particularly those on their first placement. Demystifying this process can be a major challenge for the practice educator.

Reflective journals and other tools

Reflective journals, logs or diaries are used by many HEIs to assist the student in developing their reflective skills while on placement and can prove valuable discussion tools in supervision. However, it should be noted that across the HEIs, practice educators may find that these reflective accounts are used very differently. Some students are required to submit their reflective journals (usually by email) on a regular basis to their practice educators so that they can be read prior to supervision and then used as a supervision tool to promote critical reflective discussions. Other HEIs will ask students to write the journals much like a private diary with no formal requirement to share these with the practice educator. Writing a reflective journal can prove a real challenge to students who initially tend to write a very descriptive account of their daily experiences. The provision of a journal format, which provides headings, and which promotes a reflective response, can be helpful and if such a format is not provided by the HEI then examples can be seen in texts such as Parker (2004).

Journals can prove to be an excellent tool for supporting students to explore how they might or might not have considered theory and legislation whilst undertaking their work on placement. Other tools such as case scenarios, concept mapping (literally mapping out on paper the concepts , theories and legislation underpinning your views on a case) and recent examples of SCR reports can be linked to social work style discussions. Even popular soap operas can provide interesting story lines which students can explore from a social work perspective.

Some example questions to promote the reflective process with students:

Practical Tips: Questions for students to promote reflective practice

☑ What were your planned intentions/aims when undertaking this piece of work/task?
☑ What theories, research or legislation underpinned your work?
☑ Were you successful in completing your planned work/task?
☑ If you were successful how to you know that you were?
☑ Do you think the service user feels that you were successful, if so how do you know this?
☑ Can you think of any other alternative (theories or types of intervention) you might have used in this instance? How did you decide on the option you used opposed to these alternatives?
☑ What skills do you think you used throughout this intervention?
☑ Where does your work link to the PCF or HCPC codes of conduct?
☑ Is there anything that you would do differently next time?

If, when answering these questions, your student is giving short answers which illustrate a lack of understanding of what is being examined, it may be a good idea to ask them to do some research on the purpose and models of reflective practice and present their findings to you at your next supervision session.

Small group supervision

Generally we provide supervision to our students on a one-to-one basis. While this is the advised format, other arrangements such as occasional small group supervision can be undertaken if you find yourself being responsible for a number of students. Advantages of such group work include the sharing of information, peer support and an opportunity for the group to offer an analysis of student's experiences.

However, there are also some disadvantages and barriers to achieving effective outcomes in group supervisions. Over-competiveness by some students can disadvantage and isolate others and equally there is potential for students to over rely on the more perceived 'competent' student to take the lead in answering questions. Using a group format is not an easy option for the practice educator as it will require strong planning and facilitation skills.

Involving all the students in setting the agenda and producing some ground rules prior to the session will aid a mutual understanding of what to expect. Plans for such sessions might include each member bringing along anonymized cases to present to the group with an opportunity to receive peer feedback.

Letter to students setting out expectations for group supervision

Dear Student,

Thank you for agreeing to participate in this week's group supervision session on Wednesday the 15th at 1.00 pm in Ogden building of Trinity Hall (map attached). In order to get the most from the session, I have attached a piece of research into person-centered practice. Please read it before the supervision session and consider the following questions:

- What do you think are the strengths and limitations of person-centred practice as an approach?
- Do you think it is an appropriate approach for your setting and why?
- Can you think of a time when you have taken this approach? What obstacles did you encounter? What did you feel contributed to it going well?

Please note: Considering the above questions beforehand will allow us all to come prepared to contribute fully to the session. I shall be aiming to create a space where you will feel inspired to reflect, with the support of your peers on your practice and how theory links to practice in your placement.

We will discuss and set ground rules at the beginning of the session so please do give these some thought.

I am very much looking forward to the session. Please do not hesitate to contact me if you have any questions beforehand.

Wendy

Other agenda ideas for group work include choosing a theory, for example risk or attachment, and seeking a discussion from each student about how such a topic fits within their particular service group.

Direct observations of student practice

Direct observations of a students' practice by the practice educator is a requirement of all HEIs and the minimum number of such observations and who can complete these will be outlined in the institution's placement handbook.

Direct observations should always be planned and negotiated between the student and practice educator before they take place. It is the student's responsibility to identify the piece of work they wish to be observed completing and they will need to know which areas of the PCF domains in relation to which they want to be specifically observed (although evidence of additional attainment or lack of attainment in other domains may also be secured by the practice educator during the observation, which can be included in the final direct observation report).

If this is the student's first placement, they may feel anxious about the observations. As well as general reassurances, they might require additional support, reassurance and guidance as to the type of task they might be observed completing. It is tempting for students to choose an area of practice which is within their comfort zone but we would recommend they be encouraged to choose areas which need developing or where there are gaps in evidence.

Please do also take this opportunity to remind them that the direct observations are formative assessments which are there to offer constructive feedback on areas for improvement. They are in many ways wasted opportunities if the student is allowed to simply choose areas in which they have excellent skills already. The written format of the observation will depend on the HEI and pro-forma are usually included in the placement handbook. If the OSPE model is being used then one of the observations is also usually completed by the practice supervisor. Often observations are kept to the minimum number noted in the placement handbook (usually three), but more observations can be completed particularly, but not exclusively, if an observation raises concerns or does not offer the evidence initially identified by the student.

Less formal accounts of the student's work may also be captured by colleagues and these can be extremely valuable to the practice educator but should not replace the required formal direct observations.

If an OSPE model is being used, then it is helpful to discuss the direct observations at the placement meeting. The OSPE is usually required to do the bulk of the direct observations. On rare occasions, there can be issues if the host agency is not clear that the OSPE will require access to the student interacting with service users. Sometimes the agency concerns are underpinned by apprehensions about confidentiality and/or protection of service user's rights. Such issues can usually be addressed by the OSPE and HEI during the placement meeting where the OSPE's qualifications, background and completed DBS checks are noted. Of course, the service user will always need to be made aware of who the OPSE is, and what role they are there to fulfil, so that they can either decline or give informed consent to the OSPE observing their interaction with the student.

Supervising as an off-site practice educator

The process of supervising a student as either an on-site practice educator or an OSPE will be very similar in content and also require very similar skills from the practice educator. However, there are some additional issues which an OSPE will need to consider and address. Many are of a practical nature. First, as an OSPE it is unlikely that you will have access to your own independently located offices in which to hold supervision sessions. If you work from your own home it would be inappropriate to use your home office for student supervision unless the appropriate level of insurance and risk assessments were in place and this arrangement was agreed with the placement agency, student and the HEI. Even so, this is not an option that we would recommend. Therefore the OSPE is dependent on the placement agency to provide suitable rooms for supervision and this is usually an arrangement that works well in the majority of instances.

However, if appropriate space is not available in the placement this can prove an important issue to resolve in the planning stages of setting up a placement.

Case Example: No provision for OSPE and student meeting space

I remember one such scenario when I arrived for student supervision and was directed to a small kitchen, which was also used as a thoroughfare to access the smoking area in the back yard. When I diplomatically but firmly protested, I was informed that rooms were at a premium and that throughout the duration of this placement, this would be the only place for me to use with the student.

On this occasion, with the help of the student, I was able to make satisfactory alternative arrangements through negotiations with a partner agency. I have also in similar instances gone back to the HEI and sought space within campus and booked this meeting space for the placement duration.

Off-site practice educators tend to be quite flexible and creative with regard to addressing most placement issues, however pressures to accept inappropriate supervision space should be strongly resisted. It has been known that practice educators have felt obliged to use local cafes or public areas in the absence of any obvious alternative, but such locations can lead to poor quality supervision with stunted, interrupted discussions, constant distractions and the persistent risk of breaching confidentiality (in relation to the student, colleagues, the agency and, of course, the service user's information). If space for supervision is not easily resolved and you feel that this may continue to be an issue with future placements, you may record the issues you have had in the **quality assurance in practice learning (QAPL)** feedback which all practice educators are asked to complete at the end of placements.

As an OSPE you will be usually sharing the supervisory responsibility with the work-based supervisor (WBS). The detail of how this shared responsibility will take place should be clearly explored and recorded during the PLA meeting, as discussed in Chapter 1. The requirement from the student's HEI will usually stipulate that social work students have access to weekly supervisions of at least one and a half hour's duration.

The most common arrangements agreed if an off-site model is used are for the OSPE to alternate supervision with the WBS, so that the student receives the requisite weekly session.

Again, at the pre-placement meeting the OSPE might wish to negotiate some three-way supervisions which would include the student, OSPE and WBS. The benefits of such three-way supervisions include:

1. The opportunity to explore learning opportunities.
2. Gaining feedback from the WBS.
3. Ensuring everyone is aware of progress and or outstanding issues.

Remember though that this three-way supervision will also need to be clearly recorded and notes agreed and signed by all present. Table 2.4 contains one suggestion for how you might create a timetable for two- and three-way supervisions.

Table 2.4 Suggested model of sharing supervision for an OSPE and practice supervisor

Placement runs for 70 days

Key	
	Practice supervisor supervision
	Practice educator supervision
*	Practice supervisor sits in on first half hour of practice educator supervision

Week number

1	2	3	4	5	6	7	8	9	10	11	12	13	14	15	16	17
			*				*				*				*	

Best Practice

We would recommend that at the first supervision, you take time to put all of the subsequent supervision sessions into your diaries. This saves time at the end of each subsequent supervision session, trying to allocate time in an increasingly full diary. It also minimizes the risk of the student (and perhaps you) filling your diary until there is no time for supervision. Agree at this point that if supervisions have to be changed, they are rearranged within the week and never cancelled.

3 Assessment

In this chapter, we will cover:

- Understanding the parameters of assessment, specifically the roles and responsibilities of the practice educator and those of the student.
- Formative and summative assessment – what they mean and how to conduct them.
- Best practice, such as triangulating your findings to corroborate evidence on the student's performance.
- Using observations, written work, reflective logs, assignments, supervision and other evidence to assess a student.
- The value of a student's own self-assessment.
- What is expected of you if you are asked to mark a student's academic work.
- How to obtain and use service-user feedback sensitively and ethically.

Links to the Practice Educator Professional Standards (PEPS)

This chapter will help support your learning and practice under the PEPS domains and learning outcomes for stage 1 and 2 practice educators:

A 3, 4, 5, 8
B 2, 3, 5, 7, 8, 9
C 1, 2, 3, 4, 6, 7, 8, 9, 12, 14

and additional outcomes for stage 2 practice educators:

C 15, 16
D 1, 2, 7

Also 1.1 Values for practice educators and supervisors (see Appendix 1).

Introduction

It is important to be clear about what exactly it is that we are assessing when we are considering the student's success or otherwise on placement. What we are certainly not assessing is our own ability and performance. The student passing or failing is not necessarily a reflection of the quality of your practice education. Of course, it is important that you are adequately prepared and trained, that you have an investment in the student's ability to learn and that you work hard to facilitate the students learning. Ultimately though, it is the students responsibility, with guidance and support from you, to provide evidence that they meet the requirements set out for them at pre-qualifying levels of the PCF as well as to evidence their ability to understand the codes of practice set out by the HCPC. This is a critical point as a lack of self-awareness in this area can mean practice educators having feelings of guilt or lack of confidence, blaming themselves when students fail to achieve, and they avoid difficult decisions which may lead to a recommendation of fail or refer on the placement. In the context of practice education, we are assessing against the criteria set out by the PCF. This approach of assessing against set criteria is called **criterion-referenced assessment** and differs from **norm-referenced assessment**, which entails assessing an individual against their peers as may be the case in some exams. In a practice education context, assessing against peers or against the last student you had on placement would be unacceptable. Remember, without assessing against the criteria set out by the PCF, you risk assessing your student's performance against your potentially ill-defined or vague notions of what a student at that level should or should not be able to do, or worse, against the practice of a previous student or another student on placement at the same time as yours.

Be under no illusion: you are doing no one any favours passing a student who is not able to meet all of the criteria needed for progression. You not only cause problems for the next placement or employer on the Assessed and Supported Year in Employment, who will quickly identify your shortcomings and the student's. You will also be misleading the student. They trust you, as a professional, to make a judgement about their capacity to practice as a social worker and you let them down if you assess them too leniently. It will become apparent quickly in practice and ultimately, service users may be put at risk by poorly prepared newly-qualified social workers.

This may seem daunting but remember, the responsibility is not all on your shoulders. You are part of a team. That team consists of tutors, other practice educators on previous or future placements and the student themselves, as well as professional colleagues on placement and usually service users, all of whom contribute to the student's ultimate assessment as fit to practice as a social worker. Neither are you left alone to judge what constitutes adequate practice. You have the HEI assessment criteria which will incorporate the PCF, and the midway and final reports you will write will be directly linked to the achievement of targets set out in descriptors at each level and domain of the PCF for your student (see Appendix 2).

Furness and Gilligan (2010) pointed out that the now redundant National Occupational Standards for social work, the measure against which practice educators assessed competence prior to the PCF, were flawed as a tool to measure attainment as they provided no guidance in terms of interpretations of the standards and what constituted good enough levels of achievement (Furness and Gilligan 2010). The PCF goes some way to addressing this in descriptors linked to each level of the PCF and is listed in Appendix 2.

Using formative and summative assessments

Earl (2004) describes assessment as being 'for learning' and 'of learning'. This is a useful distinction for the practice educator. Assessment for learning, or **formative assessment**, is a tool providing feedback which students can respond to and with which students may advance their learning. This ongoing assessment loop should begin before the placement starts, with the student's self-assessment of their learning needs and feedback from their academic work. It should carry on throughout until the summative assessment and recommendation in the final report. Even then, when the student has passed, one should identify areas for further learning. This kind of assessment allows the practice to offer feedback on what the student has done well and why, so that they can replicate their practice and apply it to other situations, as well as identify areas that need further work. It allows for self-assessment and adjustment of practice on the part of the student and gives the opportunity to develop their skills or update their knowledge in order to improve. Without formative assessment, the placement experience is unfair and any summative (final) assessment would not be robust.

Summative assessment is the measure of the student's learning at a given point in time and is, in the case of the placement, the final recommendation of their pass or fail. Naturally, if formative assessment is to be useful, it needs to not only be ongoing from the very beginning of the placement, but also timely. It should be given as close to the incident which is being assessed as possible. It is of little use to see a mistake in practice and leave it for two weeks until supervision to raise the issue with the student. Similarly, once a learning need is identified, so must learning opportunities be provided. In this way, the student can receive clear, honest evidence-based feedback of what they do well and of the gaps in their learning. This is then followed by learning opportunities being identified and the student makes preparations to use those learning opportunities and tries again to evidence capability. This should all be recorded clearly in supervision notes, we suggest using SMART targets as these provide an invaluable resource with which to track progress and form the final assessment report.

SMART targets

In order to be of as much use as possible, targets set for improving performance should be SMART, that is:

- **Specific:** Ensure the target is clearly defined and in small chunks. For example, 'Ensure accuracy of chronology detail with regard to the dates of house moves, in the report on the Smith family'.
- **Measurable:** Ensure you can measure when the outcome is met. For example, the chronology will match the detail and data in the historical reports.
- **Achievable:** Ensure it is a realistic target for the student. For example, if there were no record of the family moves in historical reports and no other source of data was available, it would not be achievable.
- **Relevant:** Is the target relevant to an identified proficiency (that is, one of the learning outcomes in the PCF domains) and/or the student's needs? For example, the accuracy of chronological detail is important but would be inappropriate if you were looking to improve the student's ability on domain 5 (Applying knowledge of social sciences, law, and social work practice theory) although it may be indirectly linked, that is, there may be a court requirement to have a thorough and accurate chronology; it would not be the best target to set in terms of direct relevance.
- **Timed:** Is the student able to meet the target in the time available? For example, the student has three weeks left on placement. The only records with the details of the dates the family moved is in the password-protected file of a social worker who is on annual leave for a month in Cambodia. This target is not going to work in terms of timing and another piece of work should be chosen.

The HEI quality assurance systems provide set points at which to share formative assessment and these include the PLA and the midway review as well as a number of direct observations. Take heed of our earlier point – formative assessment and feedback on progress should be ongoing and there should be no surprises at the midway review for the student.

Practical Tips: Checklist for formative assessment

☑ What PCF domain or HCPC codes of practice am I assessing?
☑ Does the student understand how they can evidence capability of that domain? (Can they choose suitable examples to demonstrate capability? Can they describe the domain and how it might apply in practice?)
☑ Has the student had adequate time and learning opportunities to demonstrate capability?
☑ If the student has not had ample time or learning opportunities, what opportunities can be arranged?
☑ If the student is demonstrating capability, what other evidence do I have to support their ability to transfer that learning/skill to other areas (for example, service-user feedback, or observation of practice by colleagues)?
☑ Have we assessed on an ongoing basis?
☑ Have we communicated errors or areas for improvement swiftly, honestly and clearly?
☑ Have we given evidence for feedback at every stage?
☑ Have we kept detailed and clear notes?
☑ Have we ensured that the notes cover what the student is doing well and specific and achievable areas for improvement are clearly articulated?
☑ What are the outstanding learning needs or areas that can be built on further?
☑ Have we set SMART targets?
☑ Have we ensured that the summative assessment contains no unexpected revelations for the student?

If done well, these formative assessments should cumulate to inform the summative assessment, that is, the assessment of the student's learning. This is, for our purposes, usually the final report where your recommendation for a pass, fail or refer is made. Ultimately, your report will feed into a larger-scale summative assessment of the student's suitability to pass the course and qualify as a social worker.

Whether formative or summative, you should strive to make your assessments objective. We all have different perspectives and therefore will make different judgements, but they must be **evidence-based and measured against the PCF levels and domains**. We must present information about what a student is doing well and where they need to improve in clear language and linked to examples. You should also give guidance as to what the student can do to improve in the areas identified, for example:

You have structured your report well, including an accurate chronology, the summary and analysis of all current assessments and the views of significant others as well as your recommendations, well done. In order to meet the standard required for a court report, you need to proof read the document and double check it for typing errors and grammatical errors. Do not rely on spell check! If you have trouble with this, please bring it to me in supervision and we can discuss where you can access further support to develop these skills.

Remember, when assessing students work, we must be aware of our own values, acknowledging and reflecting on them in order to ensure as much objectivity as is possible. Use supervision or opportunities which arise on training or in support groups, to discuss any areas which you are finding challenging and this will afford you the opportunity to ensure you can respond professionally.

Do ensure you get feedback from the student regularly on their experience of being assessed; this models good behaviour to the student in taking on feedback about your own practice and also allows you to adapt and improve your assessment skills in future.

Triangulate your findings

Shardlow and Doel (1996) recommend **triangulation** as a means of strengthening the accuracy of assessment. Triangulation is based on the premise that more than one piece of evidence from a variety of sources, often incorporating the opinion of a number of assessors, is a stronger indicator of competence than the opinion and evidence of a single assessor. The student and practice educator are encouraged to work together to find differing sources of evidence which can be measured against each other to establish a stronger assessment of ability or area of learning. For example, you might find that the student offers some thoughtful reflections and evidences a strong knowledge base for anti-oppressive practice in their learning journals. Before assessing the student as able to 'recognize, and manage the impact of [their] own values on professional practice' it would be good practice to triangulate by a direct observation of practice and perhaps gather service-user feedback to further evidence their skills. If they failed to do in practice what they can do in theory or vice versa, then they have a learning need to attend to before they can be assessed as competent.

Sources of evidence

So, what sources of evidence should you be using and encouraging the student to gather? Given the previous points about formative and summative assessment, it should be acknowledged that everything and anything that happens on placement (and in some situations out of placement) may and should be used as evidence, either of a student's strengths or learning needs. While in the main only placement-based practice is relevant, there may be occasions when something occurs out of placement which might need to be drawn into discussion with the student. These incidents tend to be those where a student's conduct may reflect negatively on the profession or undermine the public's confidence in them. For example, a student on placement in a project working with alcohol dependants had a Twitter profile picture apparently showing him under the influence of alcohol and waving a bottle of whisky around. This was a rich source of material for the following supervision session.

Case Example: Tim's social media profile

Practice educator: So, we were going to discuss domain 1, Professionalism, today?
Tim: Yes, I've gathered lots of evidence actually. I think I'm doing well on this one. I was thinking about using the fact that I always turn up on time to meetings and

supervision and I put lots of time into preparing for that. Also, I've had some really good feedback about dealing with conflict in multi-agency meetings.

Practice educator: Yes, I agree, I can see from the evidence you've brought and from feedback from colleagues and service users that you are respected in the team and you certainly behave professionally at work. I was wondering if you can think of other opportunities professionals have to build a professional persona? Perhaps thinking about alternative ways of networking other than in person for example?

Tim: Oh, yes, definitely. Facebook and so on. We had a session in uni where they told us a nurse had been criticizing a patient on Facebook and she was struck off. I agree with that, it was really unprofessional.

Practice educator: I use social networking and as you know, I use it to disseminate helpful information and keep abreast of changes in policy and so on, but can you think of other problems social networking might pose for social workers?

Tim: Erm . . . yes, what about if a service user asked you to friend them on Facebook?

Practice educator: What would you do then and why?

Tim: Well I'd be nice but explain I'm not allowed. I'd probably hide behind the policy a bit but it wouldn't be OK, it's about professional boundaries isn't it?

Practice educator: Absolutely right. That's good, it is about professional boundaries and I know you wouldn't do that. So I'm going to be a bit challenging now – have you noticed what my Twitter profile picture is?

Tim: Yes, it's a picture of a pile of social work books on a shelf.

Practice educator: What are the reasons, do you think, that I chose that picture?

Tim: Erm . . . for confidentiality, so people can't recognize you unless you told them who you are? Possibly it says something about you, you know the social work books and you're a practice educator so it says something about you as a professional, who you are, what you do whatever . . .

Practice educator: Yes, well done, those are all the reasons I chose that picture as my profile, right – here comes the big challenge. Can you show me your profile? I've seen it on Twitter because we've talked on there haven't we?

Tim: Yes, *(gets phone out and logs on to Twitter). Tim looks at his profile (him with a bottle of whisky in a club) and looks crestfallen.*

Practice educator: What is it?

Tim: Oh, God, I've just realized . . . its not good is it?

Practice educator: Well, it's not a case of good or bad, tell me what your thinking . . .

Tim: I, well, I am drunk, not really drunk but out drinking and I've obviously got a bottle of whisky there and am enjoying it!

Practice educator: Why does that matter Tim, you're not at work are you? I mean it wasn't at 2.00 p.m. on a Monday afternoon was it?

Tim: No, but this is a drug and alcohol project, I mean I'm supporting people to not use alcohol. If they saw that, well it looks hypocritical but also, well, we were talking about Thomson's PCF model in our last session and how things are normalized but they can be oppressive. I suppose, now I'm looking at it I'm thinking, well, that's it isn't it, society says using alcohol is fine and that can make it harder for people to stop when it becomes damaging, but I'm, well, I'm reinforcing that it's fine if I'm plastered all over Twitter waving a bottle of whisky about and I'm supposed to be a social worker! I feel awful, I mean, I'm mortified. I didn't think of it like that.

Practice educator: Well, do you know what, Tim? Don't feel too awful because this is your first placement and you can see that in domain 1, it says here 'with help and support you can recognize the role of the professional social worker in a variety of settings and demonstrate professionalism in terms of presentation, demeanour, reliability, honesty and respectfulness'. I would say that with very little prompting, you were able to think about your professional role and how you present yourself in a variety of settings. Also, you were able to think about whether the placement you are on makes the photo particularly inappropriate and that's a really good thing to think about. So I think you can feel good that you are thinking about these things well and because I've minuted the conversation in our notes, you can use it as evidence you are beginning to meet domain1. Now, what might you do as a result of thinking about this?

Tim: I'm going to change that photo now. Well, actually I'm going to set up two accounts like you have, I'm going to have a personal one and I'll set up tight security and a work one and I'll only put professional things on that one, like our conversations or conversations with other practitioners. And I'm definitely getting a photo of some books or something as my profile picture! Would this be a good thing to use as a reflection in my diary?

Practice educator: I think that's an excellent idea!

Table 3.1 shows a (not exhaustive) list of areas that may be used for evidence and assessment purposes.

The social work placement is challenging. Students are expected to come on placement, apply learning which, up to now may have been largely academic, learn the rules (written and unwritten) of your workplace and fit in with a new team of colleagues as well as building a productive relationship with you. This is made even more complicated and demanding by the fact that they are aware that they are being constantly observed and assessed. If handled badly, this may begin to feel like an oppressive environment very unlikely to engender learning. Part of the expectation of a professional practice educator is to contribute to their organization becoming a learning organization.

Peter Senge defined learning organizations as: 'organizations where people continually expand their capacity to create the results they truly desire, where new and expansive patterns of thinking are nurtured, where collective aspiration is set free, and where people are continually learning to see the whole together' (Senge 1990: 3).

People do not learn when they are fearful, so it is therefore essential that you are able to create a culture of learning and model practice which shows how mistakes can be learnt from and feedback is helpful, in order to enable the student to take a similarly positive approach to their development.

Only in a positive learning environment will the gathering of **staff feedback** to contribute to the assessment of students feel and be useful and unoppressive. If you have heeded the advice in earlier chapters, the staff team should be aware of the usefulness of constructive, timely feedback; they should be willing and able to offer it to the student and, ideally, the student themselves will ascertain others' views as part of their self-assessment. It is also perfectly acceptable, assuming you have an awareness of anti-oppressive practice, for you as practice educator to gather comments and feedback to contribute to your assessment. The same rules apply here, as with your own feedback though, the team should be aware that they must raise issues as they go along. It is

Table 3.1 Sources of evidence

Sources of evidence	
Formative	**Summative**
Direct observations	Final report
Staff feedback	Graded academic work/ assignments
Observations of team work	Exams
Observations of interagency work, e.g. multi-agency planning meetings/case conferences, training attended and evidence of learning from it, taking and making referrals, speaking to other organizations on the phone/sharing information etc.	
Observations by peers in the office environment, for example: • Telephone skills • Ability to safely store confidential information • Ability to support colleagues	
Service user feedback • Gathered by student • Gathered by direct observation • Gathered by colleagues	
Formal observations of practice with service users (usually a minimum of three on each placement, at least two of which must be done by the practice educator, but refer to handbook)	
Reflective logs	
Written work, e.g. reports, case notes, emails and texts	
Supervision where you may have: • Reflective conversations • Set supplementary exercises or further reading and ask for feedback	
Self-assessment	

neither useful nor constructive for a staff member to wait until the final report is being written and then present a list of complaints about the student. The complaints would be very difficult to uphold fairly as the student had not been made aware of them nor given time or opportunities to address them.

Direct observations are a set part of the placement process and the HEI usually provide the pro forma and expect the completed items to be included in the midway and final report. We have discussed observations in Chapter 2 but, as a reminder, note that most HEIs state three direct observations need to be conducted, but remember – this is a minimum. If you feel that more evidence is needed, then it is perfectly permissible to conduct more. In this event, you and the student may simply choose the three most appropriate observations for formal submission. Direct observations are a rich and useful learning opportunity for students but are often regarded with dread. The sooner in the placement the first direct observation is done, the better. This sets the scene for the student, reinforcing that formative feedback will be an ongoing and constructive part of their experience with you. In our experience, it is also the kindest way to practise as the student can be assured that, as they have been with you for such a little time, you have no set expectation of their practice and therefore this is simply a means of establishing their baseline strengths and areas for development. Another key factor in direct observations is that they are an opportunity for self-assessment. The student should be asked to write a piece in preparation for the observation, outlining what skills and/or knowledge they think they will exhibit as well as a self-evaluation afterward which can be compared with your assessment.

Service-user feedback

If applicable, service-user feedback can also be gathered here. As the observer you should, where possible and appropriate, ask the service user for feedback about their experience with the student. Just a note of caution: you and the student are there primarily to meet service-user needs; the service user is not there to meet the needs of the student. Therefore, careful thought should be given to the situation and appropriateness of using any piece of work as a direct observation, and the service user should be asked in advance for permission and in no way led to believe that not participating would have a negative effect on them.

Service-user feedback remains a requirement on social work courses and that is a positive thing. It shows respect for the service user as often the best judge of anti-oppressive/anti-discriminatory practice, and provides a valuable source of triangulation of the students and practice educators assessment.

When gathering (or supporting the student or others) to gather service-user feedback, certain points must be considered.

Ensure you seek feedback from the widest appropriate range of service users. For example, you may have a student who communicates wonderfully with the children you work with but is unable to assert themselves with the foster carer or parents. While we must be careful to not generalize and homogenize whole groups of people with the label 'service user', the fact is, different communication skills and approaches are necessary with different groups and individuals and the social work student must show flexibility in this area.

Remember also that, often, service users are accessing your service because they are in need or experiencing difficulty in some way. It seems that every service we access, be it a phone call to our mobile phone operator tor an emergency call to the police, generates a follow-up call asking for feedback. Beware of inflicting exhaustion by feedback! Show respect. The service user will quite probably have better ways of spending their time than commenting on your student's practice. Be sensitive and encourage your student to be so.

It is an indicator both of respect and of professional practice if a student accurately judges that asking for feedback is inappropriate. Be aware of the power differential. You or your student may have control over access to resources or services that the service user needs. To ask for feedback when a person would be made to feel they could only say positive things for fear of reprisals, however subtle, is unethical. Think about the timing. Perhaps it would be best to acquire feedback after the student leaves or when the piece of work is complete, but, also be aware, in these circumstances, that you may not get it – people's lives move on and, again, feedback on your student may not be their priority.

Be aware also that the service user may not understand the criteria. After all, it is not their job so they may not have ever thought about assessing practice or understand what kind of feedback you are looking to receive. It is helpful to ensure you ask clearly and in accessible language (or, if appropriate, use signing or other communication tools).

Encourage your student to be creative and think of ways of asking very young children or people who do not use formal signing or speech for example. If your audience reads and writes and you are making use of questionnaires, please take time to ensure questions are well designed and tested. Assume a response of between a third and a half of the number sent out.

When gathering feedback about students, for example if you interview a service user following a student's direct observation, take care to ensure emphasis is put on areas for further learning being as important and valuable to the student as the positives. This gives the service user 'permission' to give feedback constructively. One way to achieve this might be to ask for a three positive things about the student's practice and three areas they need to improve. If this is followed by a question at the end asking 'is there anything else you would like to add?' it assumes equal emphasis on the strengths and learning needs. Also, remember to ask for specific and evidenced comments where possible. This may necessitate you asking supplementary questions, for example, if the service user says, 'She could be a bit more respectful', you might ask, 'What specifically do you think she could do to show more respect?' This may get the response 'She should arrive when she says she will – she's often late.' In this way, you are able to gather specific and constructive feedback.

We are assuming that you have taken heed of comments earlier in the chapter and the direct observation is appropriate and you have permission from the service user for it to be observed. Even if this is the case, ask again on the day, as the service user may feel differently. Be explicit and check its OK to get feedback at the end and ask the student to leave the room while you do so. Remember also, if the service user is giving lots of positive feedback and general good comments, ask them exactly why they feel this as, with areas of learning needs, this drills down to the skills the student used rather than recording generic comments (see below).

Case Example: How to ask for service users (adult) feedback following direct observation

Practice educator: Mrs Kingston, thank you so much for letting me observe Jenny's visit to you at home. I know Jenny said earlier that she is a social work student and that I am here to watch her working and that this will help me to decide how well she is doing in her training and where she needs to improve. You said it would be ok to speak to me alone afterwards and I just want to check that this is OK?

Mrs Kingston: Yes, that's fine, and just call me Jane.

Practice educator: (*Asks Jenny to leave the room*). Jane, as I said, I am watching Jenny today and that will help me to decide how she is doing in learning to be a social worker. It is really important to us that people who know what makes a good social worker, are able to let us know where our students are doing well and equally importantly, what they can do to get even better. Could you tell me how you think Jenny is doing both in what she does well and what she could do to get even better?

Jane: She's brilliant; she's a great social worker, much better than my last one.

Practice educator: Thank you, and what exactly would you say she does or doesn't do that makes you feel she is a good social worker?

Jane: She tells me exactly what she expects, like she said you need to empty the bins every day and wash the pots up after every meal then pick up any food that's on the floor. I put it there for the dog but he leaves it sometimes. The last social worker used to just say tidy up.

Practice educator: Thank you Jane, that's really helpful. Now, it's really important that our students have areas they can work on, what do you think these would be for Jenny? What things do you think she could do better?

Jane: Nothing really, she's great, I can't think!

Practice educator: Any area at all, it really helps us as social workers to be able to think about how we can get even better.

Jane: Well, it's hardly anything; the only thing I could say really is maybe being on time more. She's sometimes late and I know it's because she's really busy so I don't mind at all. She always apologizes so it's fine.

Case Example: How to ask for service-user (schoolchild) feedback following direct observation

Practice educator: Thank you John for letting me watch that. I was very impressed with your painting! Are you still OK to speak to me for 5 minutes when Jenny goes to make us a drink?

John: Yes.

Practice educator: So you know that I am Jenny's practice educator, a bit like a teacher?

John: Yes.

Practice educator: Well, you know that teachers tell us every now and then how we are doing with our learning and how we can get better? I need to do that for Jenny and it would be great if you could help me. I'm sure that, as you have such a lot of experience of teachers, you could think of some ideas for how we can tell Jenny what she's doing well and what she can do to get even better?

John: Well, we have reports; it's like, a mark for how well your doing under each subject and then some writing saying why you're doing well or what you can do to get better.

Practice educator: That's a brilliant idea, shall we do a report? Can I borrow those pens? (*Draws a report card*) Now, what things do you think are important to put on here? What things should social workers be able to do well?

John: Look after children.

Practice educator: Great (*writes that down*), what else?

John: I suppose speak to children, you know, like them, my other worker didn't like speaking to children I don't think. And being kind.

Practice educator: Great, I've written those down. Now, what mark would you give Jenny for looking after children?

John: B. She is good at that 'cos she picked me up with the other woman when I had to go to the foster carer's and she asked me if I was OK and stayed with me for a bit. She asked me if I wanted anything and if I had any questions. I give her an A.

Practice educator: You're really good at this! Being kind . . .
John: I give her a B.
Practice educator: Great, how do you know she's kind?
John: She asks me if I'm OK and I can tell she means it. She stayed with me a bit to make sure I was ok at the foster carer's.
Practice educator: What could she have done to get an A?
John: She could buy me things! I'd like a new football!
Practice educator: *Laughs* – Well I don't know if that's allowed but I'll certainly tell her about that!

The practice educator role in direct observation

Ensure you set parameters for practice with the student before the direct observation. Consider and agree your role in the direct observation, for example, where will you sit, will you interrupt the session and interact directly with the service user for any reason, if so, under what conditions? How will you ask the student to leave the setting so that you can gather feedback?

Practical Tips: Checklist for gathering service-user feedback

☑ Has the student identified an appropriate person to ask for feedback from? (Take note of anti-oppressive practice discussed earlier.)

☑ Has the student considered what benefit there is to the service user? This may be as simple as the service user feeling they are contributing to the education of a social worker and therefore benefiting the community – but it must not extend to bribery.

☑ Has the service user been fully informed about the purposes and uses of the feedback?

☑ Has confidentiality as it applies in this setting been explained?

☑ Has the student or person gathering the feedback shown respect? For example, has the service user been thanked for their time? Were they able to choose a time, which was suitable and convenient for them?

Ensuring students use feedback constructively

Ensure your student is taught to gather and respond to feedback, which is given freely and voluntarily, for example in the form of comments to colleagues. For instance, perhaps the student could have a feedback book and ask colleagues, with the service user's permission, to write down feedback they received about the student's practice when service users say it. Perhaps a feedback book could be left out for service users to complete or a graffiti wall where pictures as well as words could be used? Of course the method of gathering feedback will depend on your organization and who uses it, but the possibilities are great.

Finally, please remember to encourage and make use of informal feedback. It is a constant source of bemusement that organizations invest so much in gathering feedback from customers via telephone polls, questionnaires, and so on, but ignore day-to-day comments and feedback given to staff. If 20 people came to the students' first group work session and the numbers dwindle significantly for the second and third session, that in itself may be a form of feedback – listen to it.

Feedback gained in this way may be discussed in supervision and utilized as part of your ongoing evaluation of the student. This is far more useful and meaningful than frantically gathering it at the end as it allows for the feedback to be acted upon and skills development to be evidenced.

Written work

Written work of any kind on placement is an excellent source of evidence of student achievement; make use of all the formal written elements of your practice as soon as you are able. Case recordings, reports and presentations are all valuable evidence of the student's ability to communicate effectively in writing and to present information accurately, and in a manner fit for the audience. For example, very different skills are needed to write a life-story book than those used to write a court report. The student should be allowed to see examples, have detailed feedback on their first attempt and, if appropriate, attend training. Many practice educators have let themselves down by

assessing the quality of report writing as very poor but, when asked, having clearly offered no guidance as to how to write in the format required. They have set up the written work as a summative rather than formative exercise, and this is unhelpful. It is easy to forget that the knowledge you have of the approach to take to written records in your organization is learned. You did not acquire this knowledge by osmosis. Take the time and care to teach your student the skill rather than just expecting them to pick it up.

There might be occasions where you have serious misgivings about the standard of written work and in this case it is helpful to ascertain the student's views and potentially encourage the student to seek support or assessment from the HEI, which will have learning support units who can give extra tuition for writing skills. It may be that there is a disability issue and it is far from uncommon to come across able, intelligent practitioners who despair at the amount of time and effort they have to put into written work to receive only mediocre marks or critical feedback. Once such issues are identified, many of these students, having been encouraged to seek support through their HEI, have a diagnosis of dyslexia or some other learning disability. While we do not suggest that all students who struggle with their written work might have learning disabilities such as dyslexia, it is our experience that a percentage of those who do have developed coping strategies and their learning disability has consequently not been diagnosed or support put in place.

One final note on using written work as evidence to supplement formative feedback; in our experience, students may communicate perfectly professionally in case recordings and when writing reports but send emails to you as practice educator or to other people, including service users, which make extensive use of 'text speak'. This is unacceptable and appears unprofessional. Good grammar and correct spelling should be a basic requirement and the practice educator should use any such incidents to discuss with the student what impression they think the recipient forms of them when they misjudge the appropriate way to communicate in writing. By way of example, the following email was sent to a practice educator from a student wishing to introduce herself and set up a learning agreement meeting:

> Hiya, Janie tells me you're my practice educator n I'm jst contacting you to set up a meeting. Have you got any dates? Id rather avoid Monday am tbh cos im out at the weekend.
>
> Cheers.
>
> Xxx

Once rapport had been built with the student, the practice educator concerned waited for an appropriate (but early) opportunity to discuss communication styles in supervision. She set up some examples for the student to assess and included a printout of the student's own email. It was done in a safe environment and with humour, and in this way allowed the student to see, in the stark light of day, the impact of her email and the poor impression it created.

As with teamwork and gathering colleague feedback, **inter-agency work** can be a valuable source of assessment material but all parties must be aware of the status of the student and the nature of the student's work as being a learning opportunity (that is, they are not to be assessed as one would an experienced practitioner). It is helpful if partner agencies and professionals can be made aware of the way in which assessment should be made and feedback given and, where appropriate, a brief exercise encouraging the student to be focused on the PCF capabilities and asking for appropriate feedback can be useful for this purpose.

Practical Tips: Joint working/shadowing on placement exercise

Student to complete:

☑ Describe the shadowing/joint working opportunity

☑ What areas of the PCF do you think might be touched on in the work you are observing?

☑ Can you see any social work values (refer to the HCPC codes of conduct) in action?

☑ Make a note of any questions you have here: (These might relate to skills or knowledge, which you are unsure about and may need to develop. You might also make notes of any questions you have for the practitioner.)

☑ What have you learned here? (You may want to note PCF domain 5 – which looks at your understanding of social work from a range of theories including: sociological, social policy, psychology, health and human growth and development as well as legal and policy frameworks.)

☑ What do you want to develop further?

Practitioner who has been shadowed to complete:

☑ Thank you for agreeing to support our student. Please give brief comments about the shadowing experience and the student's performance including the student's completion of this form.

Reflective logs

Reflective logs can be a bone of contention for students who are struggling to see the value of reflective practice and writing. While some fill in their logs diligently, others bemoan them as a waste of time; often feeling they are not a priority as 'they are not assessed'. They are wrong. The learning journals, particularly for OSPEs, are a valuable source of information about the student's learning, value base and self-assessment. They can be used as a tool to support the student, with guidance to develop reflective and critical practice, for example, being used as the basis of reflective conversations in supervision. The student's concern with prioritizing what is assessed is understandable but it may help to explain that journals are in fact assessed. Explain that the assessment is formative, it is conducted by you and that without it you will be unable to adequately write the final report, which is the summative assessment. This report is the means by which you will make the recommendation for them to pass or fail the placement.

Academic work

Many practice educators neglect to ask to see the student's **assignments**, which will have been completed prior to placement (and are being completed during placement). If this is the case, you are missing the opportunity to learn something about your student's academic ability, writing style, the values and ideas that underpin their practice.

In addition, students often feel there is a divide (and this, sadly, is reinforced by many practitioners), between what they write at university, or the theory, and what it is like on placement, or 'real life'. This is an outdated and unhelpful approach, which paves the way for practice that is neither research-minded nor critically reflective. Such attitudes therefore may lead to unsafe practice. To show an interest in your student's academic work tells that student that the link between practice and theory is strong and necessary, it also affords you the opportunity to develop the student's understanding of applying the theory they know from their studies to their roles in placement practice.

Do not be afraid of setting or conducting **further exercises/reading and so on** in supervision. Social work students often have a heavy workload, and adding to this should not be done lightly but they can be useful if you know there is a gap in knowledge or skills, which you wish to develop. We have read final reports that, for example, indicate the lack of opportunity to discuss professional boundaries with the student. There are numerous exercises and worksheets, which could have formed an exercise or discussion in supervision and provided valuable evidence of the student's abilities or learning needs.

Self-assessment

Among other tools, reflective conversations offer an opportunity for the student to share their **self-assessment** and to begin a discussion comparing your views with theirs. Achievements and learning needs can be agreed and recorded, further learning opportunities identified and targets set.

While some practice educators might require more guidance and support than others in order to do this, it is widely recognized that engaging students in this activity is in itself encouraging learning of social work skills, namely, to be able to critically reflect on one's own practice and take responsibility for one's own learning and development. Another benefit for the practice educator is that self-assessment allows you to build a more equal relationship with the student, allowing them some power and affording you opportunities to reflect on your own judgement in light of the student's opinion or explanation of their practice. In other words, assessment becomes a mutual activity which is discussed and agreed, and this is more likely to encourage the student to achieve deeper learning than simply responding to your feedback and 'doing as they are told' in order to pass.

As well as discussing the student's choice of material to evidence capability, self-assessment may be encouraged by questioning and debriefing following pieces of work.

Some examples of appropriate questions are:
- How do you think that went?
- What were your thoughts and feelings just beforehand?
- Is that what you were expecting?
- Were your initial thoughts and feelings justified?
- What do you think you did really well there?
- What do you think you would do differently if that happens again?
- Was there anything you felt stuck with or unsure of?
- What theory were you drawing on here and why?
- What laws, policy or procedure do you think underlie this piece of work?
- Which PCF domains do you think this links with?
- Having done that, are there any skills or knowledge you feel you don't yet have?

In addition, there are several points in the placement where the HEI expects formal self-assessment. These requirements differ across HEIs but might typically include:

- The student's assessment of learning needs on the PLA.
- Planning and evaluation of direct observations.
- The student's contribution to midway and final reports.

These should come with a pro forma to be found in the university's placement handbook and may easily be adapted for use in other circumstances on placement.

To encourage meaningful self-assessment, you must, as we have already discussed, start early. The student will have been told by their HEI to consider their learning needs in order to discuss them at the PLA meeting. You are encouraged to make them meaningful by using them as the basis for the planning of the initial placement activities.

An initial assessment would include:

- Checking for gaps.
- Asking where the evidence is for the statements they make.
- Showing them the assessment criteria.

Although the assessment criteria are, in effect, the PCF domains, and they should be familiar with them. Make no assumptions.

Take a blank template of the midway or final report to each supervision session (and encourage students to do the same). Make notes, allowing the student to see how they are progressing and what measurements are being used. If this is the second placement, go over learning needs identified in the previous placement report and explore the comments with the student to ensure they are accurate and exhaustive. Use these learning needs as a baseline and add to them regularly via supervision and self-assessment. Get students used to feedback being a useful tool for ongoing formative assessment and avoid students simply 'getting through' placement days and keeping their fingers crossed for a good summative assessment at end.

Tools for self-assessment

Below are some ideas for tools to encourage self-assessment.

> **Practical Tips: Post-/pre-direct observation pro forma, often supplied by HEI**
>
> ☑ Use reflective conversations and questions in supervision.
> ☑ Learning journals.
> ☑ Assignments, which are reflective – help them to choose topics and case examples and encourage real reflection.
> ☑ Encourage them to think about and learn from feedback from service users, you and other professionals in their journals and in supervision.

Marking academic work

As practice educator, you may or may not be asked to mark academic work. Marking would normally be a joint activity undertaken between you and the student's tutor. If you are asked – stay calm. The HEI simply wish to have your perspective on the content of the assignment which will usually be a case study or other piece relating to the placement. As their practice educator, you are best placed to say if you feel the student has adequately represented what actually happened and captured and articulated their subsequent learning.

This is an excellent opportunity to develop your skills and is good material for your own **continuous professional development (CPD)** registration. Do make sure you record it and add it as a new skill for re-registration with the HCPC.

If you do find yourself in the position of having to joint mark academic work and you have little or no experience in this area, ask the HEI tutor for guidance.

4 Report writing

In this chapter, we will be cover:

- Guidance on midway and final reports.
- The first placement report, its main function and audience.
- The second placement report and how it should build on, and respond to, the initial report.
- Examples of good reports, how to use appropriate and neutral language.
- Maintaining professionalism in submitting timely and accurate reports.

Links to the Practice Educator Professional Standards (PEPS)

This chapter will help support your learning and practice under the PEPS domains and learning outcomes for stages 1 and 2 practice educators:

A 3, 4, 5
B 4, 7, 8, 9
C 2, 3, 4, 6, 7, 8, 9

and additional outcomes for stage 2 practice educators:

C 16
D 3, 4

Also 1.1 Values for practice educators and supervisors (see Appendix 1).

Introduction

The main reports that concern you as a practice educator are the midway and the final report. As the titles suggest, the midway review is presented at the midway meeting and the final one at the final meeting. It is important that you understand the time frames for both reports, the required formats that the student's HEI needs, and what role the student plays in contributing to the report before you begin.

Time frames

We would advise a full draft is circulated for comments and consideration no less than a week before the meeting at which the report is presented. Amend with feedback following the meeting and circulate the final copy for agreement and signing. In the case of the midway report, this should be completed no later than a week after the midway meeting.

As regards the final report, the HEI will specify in the handbook when it must be submitted but this is often two weeks following the last day of placement.

The student's role

Different institutions will have different criteria for their reports. For example, you could find that the student is asked to complete the bulk of the midway report for you to comment on, and vice versa for the final report. With the introduction of the PCF, the emphasis is now on the student, with support and guidance, to take responsibility for the identification of evidence of their competency and for presenting that to their practice educators. Given this, it does make sense that the midway report is largely written as an exercise in self-assessment by the student, with the practice educator's comments. However, in many HEIs, the practice educator produces both reports and the student is asked to comment. It is your responsibility to find out what is expected in the reports and to plan ahead accordingly.

Whichever way it is done, as we have mentioned throughout the earlier chapters, your HEI will provide you with a placement handbook and it is common practice for templates for these reports to be in there. Higher education institutions will also provide workshops and other forms of support around completing the midway and final reports and, as suggested earlier, volunteering for practice educator panels is an excellent way of learning what constitutes a good report, which can contribute towards your own continuous professional development plan.

Second-year placements: doing some groundwork

If it is a second-year placement, it is important to consider the previous year's final report. We strongly advise you to ask for this at the PLA meeting and read it!

This report, if written well, will inform you of the students' progress so far and should influence your approach to their learning needs; you should be able to ascertain what types of learning opportunities they had, and their capability, and build on these when planning your own work with the student.

The reports are used to form a part of the assessment of student progress and as such are crucial documents. Here we look in more detail at the two reports.

The midway report

The midway report is, in essence, a progress check and it is important because it keeps both the student and the practice educator on track. Achievements and development can be identified and applauded, and capabilities that are still to be developed can be agreed with targets set to meet them in the second half of the placement. Crucially, it is also a point at which any lack of learning opportunity can be addressed as can low-level problems which the student of practice educator/practice supervisor have experienced. Although we discuss what to do when things go wrong in Chapter 6, it is helpful to remember that, often, problems or points of clarification may arise in the first half of the placement and the midway review is the ideal place to tackle them. Because the personal tutor is often present at the midway review, it is particularly helpful to clarify points on which the HEI will have the final deciding vote. For example, many HEIs incorporate study time into the placement and this might be a half day per week. The student may feel they should be able to manage their study day independently and the practice educator may feel the student is not using the time well or may wish to contact them within that time and be having problems doing so. The tutor will be able to clarify expectations at the midway review point.

Remember, identifying areas of learning need on the student's part or problems on the part of the placement or practice educator at this point will be essential should the recommendation at the end of placement be a fail or refer. If issues are clearly identified here and the student (or practice educator and placement setting) has been offered ample time and opportunities to improve, this will provide helpful evidence to the Practice Educator Panel and Course Assessment Board who will be better able to make a fair judgement.

The final report

This contains a recommendation of a *pass*, *fail* (or, in some cases, *refer* or *defer*) of placement and, subject to passing their other academic requirements, whether the student can progress to the next year of study, or in the final year, graduate.

It is tempting for students and practice educators to focus on this summative assessment but in many ways, it is the formative assessment which is of more value to the student's learning experience and it is here that the quality and accuracy of the midway report is most valuable. Even when the report is the final summative report of the last placement, there should be a strong formative emphasis. It is this document that the student and their future employers on the assessed and supported year in employment (ASYE), will refer to in order to build the student's continual professional development plan in the early stages of their career.

First-placement final reports

In this report, you are assessing the student's progress and abilities at one of the four student levels of the PCF, which are measures of capability at 'The end of the first placement' when students are expected to be able to demonstrate: 'effective use of knowledge, skills and commitment to core values in social work in a given setting in predominantly less complex situations, with supervision and support; and the capacity to work with people and situations where there may not be simple clear-cut solutions' (TCSW 2012). This report is developmental – a starting point for the next placement. It has three audiences: the student, their HEI and their next practice educator.

When writing your report, it is helpful to consider the next practice educator who, in many senses, along with the student, is the audience for whom you are writing. Too many reports make general comments or raise concerns in such a cryptic way that they are practically indecipherable.

Make the next practice educator's job easier; make the report clear. It will be used (among other things) as the basis of the student's learning needs for next placement.

Given this, it is sensible and best practice that the student is regularly involved in updates of your assessment. Nothing that is in your report should be a surprise to the student at either the midway or the final meeting.

This goes for the final report too. In extreme situations, lack of openness and transparency with the student when problems have occurred will lead to students, understandably, challenging the practice educator's recommendations. While neither author has seen this scenario in practice, it is possible that, in extreme situations, a student might start legal proceedings should significant damage be done as a result of a poorly supported recommendation to fail the student. Practice educators' employing organizations will have adequate public liability and professional indemnity insurance, but independent practice educators should ensure they have these in place to protect their interests. If you follow good report writing practice, as outlined here, you should avoid these situations. In the rare case your recommendations are challenged, the quality of your report really comes into play.

Ensuring the report is robustly evidenced

Evidence in the reports should be:

Reliable: The evidence should be in line with the holistic assessment and indicate that the student is able to replicate the learning (or transfer the learning) from one environment to another and on different occasions (re-test reliability). Different assessors, all things equal, should also produce the same assessment result (inter-rater reliability).

Valid: Are you measuring what you are supposed to be measuring and at the appropriate level? In this case, are you measuring to the PCF domains and at the required level for progression (content validity)? Does the assessment capture the values and attitudes of social work (construct validity)? Is the assessment an accurate predictor of future performance (predictive validity) (Walsh 2010)? Also, is there sufficient evidence? Note our comments on triangulation (Chapter 3, p. 38).

Practice educator panels and other quality assurance mechanisms require reports which give clear evidence of progress or lack of sufficient progress, in an honest manner and which are underpinned with examples to back up your statements. Without it, they cannot support the recommendations therein. In order for the report to be used constructively, you must record progression clearly, give examples of where the student was before, where they are now and evidence improvement. The Case Example below shows this in practice.

At the PLA meeting, Jane stated she wished to develop her report writing skills. Jane has read reports written by other social workers and has attended in-house training to develop her skills. Jane has used the skills she acquired to gather information regarding a family with whom she has worked and has taken the lead on writing the report for the case conference. Jane discussed the report in supervision and consequently reread her report, making amendments to avoid emotive language. She was then able to share the report with the family and present it at the case conference. The chair of the conference contacted the team manager commenting on the high quality of the report and the confidence and sensitivity with which it was delivered.

Finally, specify learning needs clearly. Beware of writing general comments here, for example, 'Jane would benefit from working with children in her final year' does not tell us what skills and knowledge she *needs* to build.

An example of a statement that would give a clearer idea of the learning needs would be: 'Jane will benefit from working within child protection legal framework and needs opportunity to develop her communication skills when working with children of primary school age and under, as well as the opportunity to develop her knowledge of child development'.

If the student has met the capability requirements for first placement, they may progress to the next level. The assessment and report writing must develop as the students prequalification experience develops and The College of Social Work (TCSW) notes that progression between levels 'is characterised by development of people's ability to manage complexity, risk, ambiguity and increasingly autonomous decision-making across a range of situations' (TCSW 2012).

Second-placement reports

It is important that the student's progression is mapped in each report and that it is clear whether or not the student is attaining the level of achievement expected on each placement. The student must understand the expectations of their capabilities will rise as they progress.

At second placement (or end of last placement/qualifying point), they should have:

> demonstrated the knowledge, skills and values to work with a range of user groups, the ability to undertake a range of tasks at a foundation level and the capacity to work with more complex situations. They must be able to work more autonomously; while recognising that the final decision will still rest with their supervisor, they will seek appropriate support and supervision. (TCSW 2012)

For example, take the PCF Capability under 'Contexts and organisations', which states the student must be able to 'proactively engage with colleagues, and a range of organisations to identify, assess, plan and support the needs of service users and communities'.

At first-placement level, evidence may include the student engaging in an informed discussion of a family's needs and the potential for the involvement of other services with a more experienced colleague. The student may then co-work the case, perhaps supporting the practical work of the colleague. They may, for example accompany the service user to appointments with other agencies and be able to clearly record the event and share information appropriately.

On a second placement, once the practice educator is satisfied of the student's ability, they may reasonably be expected to be the lead worker, assessing need and devising the inter-agency plan using supervision to check their thinking. They may facilitate multi-agency meetings, for example, a Common Assessment Framework (CAF), to plan and meet the needs of the service user. They might then be responsible for the writing up of the report or plan.

This second report is used, along with academic progress, to assess the student's capability to progress to practice and the ASYE year. In order to be successful, the

student will have evidenced ability in each of the domains at the final student level 'end of last placement/completion of qualifying programmes' (see Appendix 1). While there are clearly summative elements (failing to evidence their ability would mean the student had, in effect, failed the course) it is important that the formative nature of the report is not neglected. You should record clearly the attainments and learning needs which will be used as the basis for the student's own continuing professional development, starting in their newly qualified, ASYE year.

Dealing with students who fail their placement

Crucially there will be a number of students each year who do not pass their placement and cannot therefore graduate. See Chapter 6 for information about managing when things go wrong or when students are not on track to pass. However, in brief, if all has been tried and the student is not achieving a pass level by the end of placement, the formative nature of your report is particularly important. We would suggest it could go a long way towards achieving a 'constructive' fail rather than students simply walking away feeling they have gained nothing from their experience. If a student has not achieved a pass, a constructive fail is not just an idealistic standpoint. While it is more gratifying to you as a practice educator to feel that the student has had a constructive experience despite failing, it is also important to realize we do not do this just 'because we are nice people'. A constructive fail has a specific purpose; students who have not passed the course may gain more work experience and try again at a later date, and your report will be the starting point for their assessment. Alternatively, a realistic appraisal following the disappointment of not passing a course may lead them to a different profession to which they are better suited. A balanced representation of their strengths and learning needs in your report may help identify an alternative career or study route. Either way, service users will benefit from a suitably qualified and able workforce.

The structure of the report

The College of Social Work holds the PCF around which the report should be written. The HCPC defines the standards of proficiency (see Appendix 2). This is a change from the previous key roles and units which students previously met for the GSCC. While the capabilities of the PCF have strong parallels with the now defunct competencies of the GSCC, the fundamental shift is that the assessment, and therefore the report, now takes a more holistic, integrated approach to the acquisition, development and application of skills and knowledge. The PCF areas are used as overarching capabilities, which you must show the student has attained on placement. You should be satisfied that learning is meaningful and transferable. This is a move away from a tick-box approach which, some argue, the old key roles encouraged.

What remains the same are the fundamental principles of report writing in social work. Although many practice educators are apprehensive about these particular reports, it might help to remember that as a professional, you might have had training and very probably already write or contribute to reports as a part of your job. The principles in the student's midway and final report are no different and we shall recap on them here:

Practical Tips: Reports must be:

- ☑ Evidence based
- ☑ Robust
- ☑ Give examples to support statements
- ☑ Spell-checked and proofread
- ☑ Within the correct word count
- ☑ In line with your HEI's required report structure
- ☑ Clear in identifying any third party contributions which may be included
- ☑ Note AOP/ADP
- ☑ Clearly record a pass/fail (or refer is applicable)
- ☑ Signed and dated
- ☑ Handed in on time.

Best

Practice

The HEI for which you are producing the report will usually advise you about its length and structure. Most emulate TCSW's template which contains:

- A very brief (150 words) section about the nature of the placement and the student themselves; for example:

> The placement is a drug and alcohol treatment centre. It is a registered charity situated in the centre of a northern town with a multi-ethnic, diverse population. Self-referrals as well as referrals from other organizations are taken. It offers support to people wanting to withdraw completely from alcohol or drug use and to those who aim to maintain use as safely as possible. The organization works closely with housing and employment services, and has a number of approaches including group work, individual counselling and prescription services.
>
> The organization has an outreach team and a service team. Each team has seven employees from multidisciplinary backgrounds and one manager, one of whom is a qualified social worker and the other a nurse.

Do be aware here that some HEIs wish the placement organization to be anonymized and, if this is the case, this extends to your report.

- Approximately 500 words giving an overview of the students capability. An example is provided below:

> 'Jenny has proved so far to be a conscientious student. She has engaged fully in induction, training opportunities and supervision. In all instances, she contributes intelligently to discussions and exhibits a service user centred approach to practice. In supervision, she devised a template for our use where she has listed the domains

and we discuss her development under each one using examples from her placement experience.' (*Supervision notes/reflective journals*)

'Jenny is able to take responsibility for her learning and development. For example, she questions appropriately and is equally able to ask for guidance when she feels she has met the limits of her own professional knowledge. In one such instance, Jenny observed a case conference and she felt that the Independent Reviewing Officer (IRO) did not allow the social worker to fully explain her decisions. Afterwards, Jenny was able to ask the social worker how she had felt and expressed concern that if this had been her, she may have argued with the IRO in that public setting. Jenny was able to understand differences in professional approach following that discussion and this was evidenced in supervision where we discussed the incident. Jenny also realized her knowledge of the role of IRO was limited and she was able to request a meeting with the IRO service to learn more about their role.' (*Supervision/colleague feedback*)

'Jenny is a popular member of the team. She has brought a refreshing enthusiasm for the work, and is always willing to offer help to her colleagues when needed. Jenny needs to ensure that this is not at the expense of her own work and that she manages her own workload well. We have discussed Jenny bringing her workload to me for us to look at together should she feel she is struggling to say "No" to people. Finally, Jenny has a strong service-user centred approach and her commitment to AOP is clearly evident. This has won her some very positive feedback from service users, who comment she is "Not patronizing but makes me feel I can do things myself. I know she wants the best for me".' (*Supervision/service user feedback*)

'Jenny identified linking theory to practice as one of her learning needs at the PLA meeting. Jenny did struggle with this initially and while she was able to discuss theory, she found it less easy to see the practical application. She has adapted her learning journals and now explicitly identifies theoretical approaches when she examines practice. In addition, she has engaged in concept-mapping exercises in supervision which have helped her to be able to see particular interventions and approaches in practice. Jenny clearly evidenced this when she and a family support worker were assisting at a group-work session. Jenny was able to describe in clear terms, the model of group work which they were engaging in and the family support worker telephoned the office afterwards to thank Jenny for her support.' (*Supervision/learning journals/colleague feedback/group work evaluation*)

'Jenny has been consistently punctual and reliable, and has an open and honest approach to practice. She makes a professional impression in her dress, conversation and conduct and is a good ambassador for the service.'

- Roughly 250 words of commentary per PCF domain. We give one example of this, below, in reference to professionalism:

1. Professionalism: Identify and behave as a professional social worker, committed to professional development

'Jenny has engaged enthusiastically in induction and training in the first weeks of placement. The team feedback that she has been able to ask appropriate questions about their roles and interventions. Jenny has used that information to identify rich learning opportunities, which she brings to supervision to discuss.' (*Learning journals/colleague feedback*)

'In supervision, Jenny has been well equipped and contributes to the agenda. The combination of her punctuality and reliability in handing in her learning journals and her increasing ability to engage in reflective discussion mean that Jenny is developing a critically reflective approach to her own practice.' (*Learning journals/supervision*)

'In her placement learning agreement, Jenny had identified time management as a learning need. She has been encouraged to manage her own diary and learnt to use the online diary so that her colleagues could access her movements each day. Jenny has double booked two appointments but on both occasions was quick to realize and rectify the situations. She apologized to both parties and I was pleased to see that she prioritized the service user's appointment over the professional's when rescheduling. In addition, Jenny was able to reflect on the incidents in supervision and realized she needed to synchronize her diary as soon as she returned from her study day (as other staff put in appointments for her). She rectified this and since then there have been no more incidents of double booking.' (*Practice supervisor feedback*)

Note in this example, the sources of evidence have been included in italics in brackets.

- Approximately 200 words on their future learning needs and priorities. Here is an example of how you might frame this part of the report:

'Jane will benefit from working within child protection legal framework. She also needs the opportunity to develop her communication skills when working with children of primary school age and under, as well as the opportunity to develop her knowledge of child development.' (*Supervision/learning journals/direct observation*)

When commenting on the areas above, you must use evidence to support the opinions you are putting forward. This evidence may take the form of an observation of practice, feedback from a colleague or service user, or any other forms of evidence gathered (see Chapter 3 for more information about what constitutes appropriate evidence).

Remember, in the PCF, the capability is being evidenced across different domains and so, in order for evidence to be robust, it is helpful if you give examples and evidence from a variety of sources and different situations. For example, if you were to write that student X has evidenced good practice in their communication, you might say:

- *how* it has improved
- *what* theory they have used to develop their skill
- *where* you have seen them use this skill (using a number of different areas, that is, in writing, spoken work, and with children and adults)
- *who* observed and evaluated the practice (triangulate by gathering from a range of places, for example, service-user feedback, colleague feedback or practice educator at direct observation).

For example:

> 'Jenny stated at her placement learning agreement that she wanted to develop her communication skills. She has been able to read theories of communication and has used them in concept maps in supervision with regard to her assessment. Furthermore, she attended training around communicating with young children and managing conflict. I observed her implementing the communication skills in her one-to-one work with children (see direct observation), and children's feedback included lovely images of them smiling and sitting on the floor talking to Jenny. She was able to test her skills in managing conflict in her group work with adults where feedback from her co-worker was that "Jenny impressed me with her use of mediation, implementing it when two parents were in conflict. She calmed the situation". In addition, I observed her calm a distressed mother in reception until the appropriate worker was found.'

As with your case recording or report writing in other areas, please do ensure you leave time following completion of the report to revisit it and check it for an oppressive and discriminatory tone or inappropriate use of language. It is easy to allow personal rather than professional judgement to influence practice and this is often evident in use of language. For example, a student and practice educator were struggling to work constructively together. After some discussion about the root of the problem, the student said she felt that the practice educator did not trust her. The practice educator was shocked and disputed this. On looking at the supervision notes, the practice educator had asked the student if she had written her learning journals in one sitting just before they were due in. She had recorded the student's response thus: 'When challenged about when she wrote her learning journals, Sarah claims she writes them at the end of each day rather than writing them just before they are due in.' Here, use of the word 'claims' infers distrust and became the root of several issues which had to be resolved during that placement. It may have been better to write: 'Sarah explained she writes them at the end of each day.'

This is a good reminder of how our values and assumptions may be reflected in our use of language. It is often helpful to leave enough time after completing a report to revisit it and check for neutrality of language. It is very easy to transfer our emotions or frustrations onto the page but such practice may be perceived as oppressive and will certainly damage the relationships between practice educator and student.

Submitting the final report

One of the areas in which you are assessing the student is professionalism, and another is intervention and skills. Please, then, ensure your own report is checked for spelling and grammar.

Remember that you are modelling good practice and to submit a report of poor quality undermines the quality of your teaching and your professionalism. Similarly, students are expected to evidence that they can work to agreed time limits (again, this may be evidence of professionalism in the language of the PCF), and you should also

endeavour to do this. Apart from reflecting poorly on your professional practice, submitting a late report can have other repercussions. Please do give a thought to the student who has to wait much longer than their peers to confirm they have passed the course or can move to the next year.

This can be extremely stressful and in a worst-case scenario, may block their progress if exam boards to not have the necessary information with which to ratify a pass.

If you have followed the advice in this book you will have brought the report templates to supervision, have made notes and discussed progress with your student throughout. With all of that information in place, a good report should take an experienced practice educator about six hours to get it to a full draft to be circulated to the student and, if appropriate, the work-based supervisor for comment. Following the midway or final meeting, leave about an hour to make any amendments or additions and the report can then be circulated for approval and signatures.

Obtaining signatures

Once all the hard work is done and you are happy with your report it is essential it is signed and dated. In order to be valid, signatures are required. *If it isn't signed and dated, it isn't done!*

A word of warning: it is worth checking at the final meeting that all parties have electronic signatures and if not, negotiate how and when the report will be signed.

It cannot be stressed enough how much time, energy and fuel we have seen wasted by frantic practice educators trying to gather signatures from all parties once placements are finished. This is especially true of off-site practice educators who may have to travel some distance to meetings and do not see the student and practice supervisor every day. Spare yourself the stress and arrange how the signatures are to be obtained at your final meeting if possible.

The QAPL form

Last but certainly not least, do get into the habit of submitting the QAPL form (see Chapter 5) with the final report. This form is often overlooked or done as an afterthought but it is an essential part of the quality assurance process and your professionalism in completing and returning them will not go unnoticed by the HEI.

A time line for the submission of reports

See Table 4.1.

In summary, when report writing you should:

- Understand the aims of each report at each stage of the placement process.
- Understand what the student's HEI requires in terms of content, structure and time lines.
- Communicate the content of your report at all stages with your student.
- Plan ahead for the report deadline and allow sufficient time to write your report.
- Consider the multiple audiences – student, HEI staff and future practice educators.
- Write clearly, honestly, and with a robust evidence base.
- Map your comments explicitly on to the PCF.
- Use neutral, non-discriminatory language.
- Spell check, proofread and format the report clearly.
- Ensure all necessary signatures are obtained ahead of deadline.
- Submit on time.
- Review the report with your student whether pass or fail.

Table 4.1 A time line for submitting a final report

	1 week before – circulate full draft of midway report for comment/consideration	1 week after – circulate final version for signing	At least one week before – circulate full draft of final report for comment/consideration	2 weeks after (or length of time specified by HEI), submit final signed version to HEI
PLA	Midway meeting		Final meeting	
Ask to see previous placements Final report (if applicable)	Note amendments/additions		Note amendments/additions	

5 Quality assurance

In this chapter, we will be covering the following:

- The context of quality assurance processes.
- Quality assurance in practice learning procedures which you will work with as practice educators.
- How to create an environment where students feel they can give honest feedback about their placement experience, including your practice education.
- How to encourage consistency of quality when working with third-party feedback on the student's performance (including service-user feedback).
- What to do if you can no longer deliver a high-quality placement or supervision experience.

Links to the Practice Educator Professional Standards (PEPS)

This chapter will help support your learning and practice under the PEPS domains and learning outcomes for stages 1 and 2 practice educators:

A 4, 6, 7, 8
C 11, 12, 13

and additional outcomes for stage 2 practice educators:

D 1, 2, 3, 4

Also 1.1 Values for practice educators and supervisors (see Appendix 1)

Introduction

Higher education institutions have an obligation to a number of agencies for quality assurance. At time of going to press, these agencies include the Quality Assurance Agency (QAA), the HCPC and the **TCSW**. Although criticized as cumbersome, in the absence of a current alternative, adherence to these varied standards and their measurement criteria are necessary to maintain public confidence in standards in relation to social work education. These processes and procedures include quality assurance systems, which are used to establish and monitor standards of teaching and assessment.

For social work courses, this obligation extends to placements, although Croisedale-Appleby, D. (2014: 53) states it is 'unclear whether QAPL (SfC and TCSW 2012) impacts upon the quality of Placements, or merely monitors them, and the processes should be further improved in their rigour and usefulness'.

As a practice educator, you will come into contact with quality assurance systems on the monitoring of social work placement opportunities via quality assurance benchmark systems, or QAPL procedures.

The first contact the practice educator has with QAPL forms is usually at or before the PLA where the HEI tutor will bring the 'practice learning opportunity audit form'. It is generally the tutor's role to complete this but they will ask for information from the practice educator. Some basic facts are gathered, such as name and contact details of organization as well as whether the placement is an adults' or children's setting. Following that, the nature of the questions centre around whether the staff allocated to practice educate/workplace supervise are suitably qualified and whether the placement will provide all the necessary learning opportunities for the student to have the opportunity to demonstrate capability in the PCF domains.

At the end of the placement, practice-learning questionnaires are filled in by both the student and the practice educator. The practice educator questionnaires ask for feedback about the readiness of the student at the beginning of placement and the level of information and support provided to you by the HEI, as well as the support you receive from your organization for your role as practice educator.

The student form asks for feedback about the quality of the placement processes and procedures. This ranges from allocation of placement by the HEI through to the quality of the placement experience itself, including the work of the practice educator.

The importance of the QAPL forms cannot be stressed highly enough. It is understandable to see practice educator and/or student get to the end of the placement and neglect these forms, feeling that they are administrative and that as the placement has ended, so has their involvement. Not so! The information from these forms is essential to the HEI in ensuring high-quality placements are supported and maintained, and are used to ensure students are matched to appropriate placements in future years. In addition, the form is a useful tool for you to use in assessing your own practice and that of your organization, evidencing you are able to contribute to your place of work as a learning organization; this is an area of assessment you will need to demonstrate if you undertake the practice educator award.

Whistle-blowing

A word on the QAPL forms; in the unusual event of serious concerns being raised by the student, do not wait until the end of the placement to raise the issues on a QAPL form. A critical incident on placement which impacts negatively on service users must be addressed as a matter of urgency and in exceptional circumstances will require the student to access whistle-blowing procedures. For example:

> Jane is upset in supervision and discloses she has seen a staff member handle a service user roughly while assisting him in and out of his wheelchair. She feels bad because she has not mentioned it before. She raised it today because, she says, it happened again. This time, the man shouted and the worker pushed him in response.

> The practice educator reassures Jane that she has done the right thing in raising this issue and together they look at the whistle-blowing policy. As a result of this, the practice educator supports Jane to record the incident and report it to the manager of the setting.

Depending on the outcome, the practice educator should discuss with the HEI whether the placement continues to be an appropriate and safe setting for the placement to continue.

Critical incidents such as this aside, if elements of the placement or relationships between student, HEI and placement have been characterized by significant (but less serious) problems, say so. It can be difficult for all parties to formally record issues which may have arisen, but it benefits future students, the HEI and the placement setting if you do so. Naturally, it can be difficult to hear less than positive feedback. The HEI, for example, might have concerns about hearing criticism about the quality of their handbook as this might necessitate someone being allocated the job of amending it. Placements might be concerned that they will not be asked to host students again if they comment that they were not prepared well enough for placement; students may complain of inconsistent supervision. Unless all parties are prepared to resolve the issues as the placement progresses or raise this in their QAPL feedback, those problems will go unrectified and be compounded year on year. Students in the past have reported not being willing to record concerns on their QAPL forms, fearing they would be branded a troublemaker and this would go against them when they applied for their second placement or wished to apply for jobs on graduating. It is essential that the practice educator models responsible, professional behaviour in giving and receiving feedback, these forms may be brought to supervision and used as reminders of what is expected and what standards we are working to.

Common
Pitfalls

Case Example: Encouraging student to give feedback on QAPL

Practice educator: John, we've gone through your final report and I wanted to remind you that you have to fill in the QAPL form. I have brought it with me in case you have any questions but most students complete it alone and submit it straight to the university.

John: (*laughs*) Yes, I've been kind of putting that off! I mean there were problems at the beginning with the misunderstanding about supervision but it got sorted out when you spoke to the practice supervisor so I don't think I need put it down. (*Pauses*). It was just the other students I was thinking of. I don't think theirs got sorted out.

Practice educator: Well, you are right in that you can't speak for other people but I think your experience was really helpful. Feedback on QAPL forms helps us as practice educators to improve, and the same goes for placements. You know from your PCF domains that as social workers we all need to be able to develop our practice, even when we've qualified. Listening to feedback is part of that.

John: (*laughs*) Well, yes, on paper but I have to try to get work in this authority!

Practice educator: (*laughs*) Well, that's a good point. Seriously, as an employer, I'd rather employ a social worker who I know is able to present information which may be difficult to hear in a really helpful and constructive way. I'd also want to employ

> people who could contribute to my organization as a learning organization and be able to give and receive feedback. How about if you talk through how you might present what you want to say in a really constructive way?
>
> **John:** Yeah, that would be helpful. I do think it would be helpful if they could sort out the supervision for students and other people don't have to struggle like I did . . .
>
> **Practice educator:** I think that's a good decision. And remember when you have thought about how to present information, I hope you will feel really confident in feeding back to me any areas where you think I could improve in my practice educating. It really helps me as a social worker and practice educator to be able to reflect on and try to improve my own practice.

Reminding the student of your wish to receive feedback and your ability to respond to it appropriately can be a valuable way to redress the power imbalance and support students who feel overwhelmed by the idea that they are being assessed continually.

Other uses for the QAPL form

Should your student not be progressing, it may be useful to check together that both of you agree that the areas covered in the QAPL forms have been met. Sometimes it pays to go back to basics.

> In the days of predominantly paper-based recording systems, I knew a student who did not provide any evidence of her ability to take case notes despite being asked to do so in supervision. We revisited the QAPL only to find that she had had no formal induction, she had not been shown where the paperwork and templates for files were kept and had been too embarrassed to ask the rather brusque administration manager. An extreme example, admittedly, but one which could have escalated into a bigger problem had we not revisited the basics by referring to the QAPL form.

Of course, if we are to ask for feedback about the quality of our organization as a placement provider, and of our own abilities as practice educators, then we must be prepared to act on that feedback. If you are undertaking the practice educator award, the feedback will prove useful in evidencing your ability to develop your own practice. You may have already done the awards or aim to do them in the future, and feedback from students can be a useful tool to take to your own supervision to discuss training needs, additional support or areas of expertise which you have developed and which you wish to use in your organization.

Most HEIs welcome a partnership approach to practice educating. Many placements make use of partner agencies to allow students to shadow colleagues from other settings and, indeed, engage in joint pieces of work. With such arrangements, it is the practice educator's responsibility to ensure the partner agency and the student are aware that the same quality benchmarks are expected in relation to the pieces of work. It is advisable, for example, to remind the student and the other professional of when and how the student will be assessed and that time spent with colleagues in other settings will form a part of their assessment for which feedback will be sought. Likewise, the professionals giving the feedback need to be reminded of the need for it to be clear, fair and evidence based. (See the shadowing form in Chapter 3.)

Colleagues and service-user feedback

You can avoid the pitfalls of not being clear about when and how students will be assessed by being constructive, open and honest throughout.

Case Example: Colleagues and service-user feedback

I recall one particularly heated telephone call from a distressed student for whom I was off-site practice educator. The student called late one afternoon in a distressed state saying she would not go back to placement as she had discovered her practice supervisor had been 'talking about her behind her back'. After calming the student down and asking further questions, it transpired that the practice supervisor had asked colleagues with whom the student shared an office, how they felt the student was settling in and specifically if they were aware of any problems. It took me a significant amount of time to calm the student and remind her of the placement learning agreement where we noted the nature and methods of assessment that were open to the practice supervisor to use.

This could have been avoided had the student had a supervision session discussing the benefits of feedback and how to respond to it constructively. She could also have been reminded more clearly and frequently of how and when she would be assessed, and perhaps been more in control of the request for and collection of feedback.

Collecting feedback from service users can be even more challenging. The practice educator is encouraged to take note of best practice outlined in Chapter 3. In addition, it is advisable to assure yourself of the student's understanding of and respect for anti-oppressive practice and social work values before sharing service-user feedback with the student. Service users may feel inhibited about giving feedback about the quality of a student's practice (or a worker's, for that matter) owing to concerns that any less than positive comments may negatively influence the service they receive in future. It is essential that the practice educator can encourage and support service users to give honest, evidence-based feedback, but also to ensure that the student understands the value and use of that feedback and that their professional relationship with the service user will not be affected.

What if you cannot deliver?

We hope that your placement runs smoothly and you are able to perform the role of practice educator confidently for its duration. However, this is not always possible. Organizations are not static and circumstances may change as placement progresses.

Staffing changes and changes to funding are two of the areas which may impact on the smooth running of the placement. If these affect your organization and you find you are struggling to support the student placement as you had intended, the matter must be addressed and HEI and quality assurance processes can be invaluable in helping this. Contacting your HEI representative, in most cases the student's personal tutor, and notifying them of the situation is the first step. From here, the tutor will support you to find a solution to the problem. It is advisable that you use the PLA and the QAPL forms to self-assess those areas, if any, in which you are still able to support the student. The HEI would much rather you come to them with an honest appraisal of the situation for resolution rather than wait and waste the student's placement time hoping matters will resolve themselves.

Common

!

Pitfalls

Case Example: Dealing with problems within the team where a placement is being hosted

Scenario 1
During placement, the practice educator's post is cut, owing to funding problems, and the practice educator is relocated. A solution is sought immediately. The practice educator contacts the tutor and explains the situation. Following discussion, the practice educator contacts the team they were relocated to and discovers they are approved placement providers. The practice educator requests that the student moves with her to the new team, which is identified as being appropriate for continuing and building on the skills and experiences the student has gained so far (the move was from a hospital team to a discharge team in the community).

Scenario 2
The practice educator's team is merged with another and some staff posts were made redundant. Cases increase and the practice educator has to take on more casework. He finds himself unable to meet his obligations to the student with regard to supervision and general support. The matter is left and the student feels unable to raise her concerns, as she is aware of the pressure the practice educator and wider team are under and does not want to add to it. The tutor is not made aware of the situation until the final meeting when the practice educator does not produce the final report, and the student breaks down crying, revealing how vulnerable and unsupported she has felt. The practice educator subsequently takes sick leave and an off-site practice educator is employed to gather as much information as possible from the team and do some additional assessments in order to submit the final report, which the original practice educator had in draft.

Time, money and upset could have been spared had the practice educator and student contacted the HEI tutor earlier.

In Chapter 7, we recommend you volunteer for **Practice Educator Panels (PEPs)** and to act as moderator if the opportunity arises. We reiterate that here and promote participation in PEPs as a means of further understanding how quality assurance systems are utilized in the assessment of placement reports and portfolios.

Figure 5.1 is an example of the placement allocation and monitoring process, as a recap of the quality assurance process.

Placement Allocation & Monitoring Process

Student completes Placement Application Form (PAF) which details their work experience, education history and their individual learning needs.

Placement Coordinator undertakes placement matching taking into account individual student circumstances and learning needs. PAFs then sent out to specific agencies.

Agency considers student PAF for suitability and if they are happy to proceed the student contacts the agency to arrange an informal meeting.

The Informal Meeting/Interview

The student has the opportunity to learn more about the placement and available learning opportunities. The meeting allows both the student and the placement provider to consider the appropriateness of the allocation (HEI QAPL completed).

The Pre-Placement Meeting

A meeting between the student, practice educator, work-place supervisor (if applicable) and the HEI tutor. This is an opportunity clarify the roles and responsibilities of everyone involved in the placement and complete the Student Learning Agreement.

The Mid-Placement Review

A meeting between the student, practice educator, work-place supervisor (if applicable) and the HEI tutor. This is an opportunity to discuss the progress a student is making towards gaining evidence of capability in relation to the PCF. It is also an opportunity to check if the opportunities agreed in the practice learning agreement are still appropriate and whether it is necessary to amend the agreement. It is an opportunity to reach an agreement about what needs to happen in the second half of the placement.

The Final-Placement Review

A review between the student, practice educator, work-place supervisor (if applicable) and the HEI tutor. This is an opportunity to discuss the progress that the student has made and the recommendation that the practice educator is making about practice (pass/fail). This is also an opportunity to discuss the student's future learning needs.

Student and Practice Educator Feedback (QAPL form completed and sent to HEI).

Figure 5.1 Placement Allocation and Monitoring

6 If things go wrong

In this chapter, we will be covering the following:

- Exploration of where problems with placement might first be identified.
- An overview of the types of problems students might face while on placement.
- The practice educator student relationship.
- The process for managing problems which persist.

Links to the Practice Educator Professional Standards (PEPS)

This chapter will help support your learning and practice under the PEPS domains and learning outcomes for stage 1 and 2

A 4, 5, 7, 8
B 3, 7, 8
C 9, 10, 11, 13, 14

and additional outcomes for stage 2 practice educators:

D 3, 4, 7

Also 1.1 Values for practice educators and supervisors (see Appendix 1).

Introduction

In the main, practice educators will find that the majority of social work placements progress with very little difficulty and prove to be positive experiences for all concerned. However, in some instances problems can occur but most will be relatively straight-forward to address. More serious or complex problems can result in placement terminating and/or the practice educator having to recommend a student has not reached the required standard to either progress to their next year of study or, in the case of final year students, the recommendation may be that the student has not reached the required level of capability to qualify.

Placements are experiential, an opportunity for social work students to apply theory secured in the classroom setting to practice with service users. This process can test a student's practical and academic skills and knowledge, and can provoke a wealth of responses, some of which may challenge the student's values, and beliefs. The range of problems that can occur on placement can manifest at any stage of the placement. They might be problems relating to the student's capacity or capability, but it is important to keep an open mind and acknowledge the problems may also be rooted in the placement organization or the behaviour of other professionals therein. Some issues can be addressed with minimal efforts while other, more complex, issues can require longer-term management. Managing difficult placement problems can be a complex task for practice educators and might prove stressful and emotionally draining, particularly when having to raise serious concerns. The student themselves often will identify the issue and seek out support and guidance. In other instances students may not have insight into the presenting issue(s) or may find it difficult to share concerns owing to fears relating to issues of power imbalance or fears of failing their placement. It is the role of the practice educator to identify in a timely fashion any placement problems and to then work openly and honestly with the student, providing guidance and support to them. Situations where problems or difficulties might be identified include:

- Pre-placement meeting (for example, concerns might be raised while talking with a student about their lack of basic understanding of the expectations placed upon them. How the student presents in these early stages, for example indicating a lack of apparent motivation, may cause concerns)
- Placement agreement meeting (for example, discussions may raise issues/conflicts around start and end times, working day or lack of relevant learning opportunities)
- Supervision (for example, the student might share issues openly or the practice educator might identify through ongoing discussions that a student is experiencing oppressive behaviours from other professionals)
- Reflective journals (for example, issues relating to conflicting values/beliefs, lack of progression or understanding about practice requirements or values)
- Direct observations (for example, practice educator notes lack of student's inability to gain from learning despite support and the setting of clear achievable targets)
- Feedback from colleagues (for example, concerns about the student's ability to comply with agency policies and procedures).

Reasons why placements might become problematic

Issues owned by the student:

- **Personal issues** – for example, relationship breakdown, housing/financial issues, bereavement, changes in physical or mental ill health.
- **Level of ability** – the student may not have acquired sufficient underpinning understanding of theory, skills or legislative knowledge to effectively work with the service-user group at the required level for their stage on the course.
- **Unprofessional behaviour, misconduct and or dangerous social work practice** – for example, lack of punctuality/attendance, failing to adhere to agency policy and procedures, inability to maintain professional boundaries. A DBS is completed prior to placement and it is the responsibility of the student to inform their tutor/HEI of any changes; failure to do so would constitute a serious concern.
- **Academic issues** – outstanding academic assignments from previous taught sessions can add to pressure on the student during placement. Alternatively, unaddressed issues such as dyslexia might be a barrier to the student's ability to deliver acceptable written work.

Issues owned by others:

- **Bullying, oppressive or discriminative behaviours** – a student experiencing oppression and or discrimination either in the relationship with their practice educator or within the wider placement environment (see Chapter 2).
- **The student not being adequately prepared by HEI for placement** resulting in issues such as lack of awareness of expectations, lack of opportunity to explore own values and beliefs.
- **Underpinning agency issues that impact upon its ability to provide the student with a positive learning experience** – for example, significant changes to funding arrangements, redundancies, changes to location and staffing issues.
- **Problems with the practice educator's own professional development or support systems** – consequent inability to provide an effective learning environment.

Any of the above issues could impact on a student's ability to meet the required standards while on placement. The practice educator will need to ensure that they are able to remove barriers to the student's learning. Tools that can help the practice educator with such a task include learning styles exercises (see Chapter 2) and any practice educator can develop skills audits such as the simple exercise in the Case Example and Figure 6.1 below. This example encourages students to self-assess their current skills and rate of progress or indeed lack of progress over an agreed timescale. Involving the student in self-assessment of practice can help with making effective plans to start to address difficulties. Scaling exercises completed by both the practice educator and the student can identify any areas where the practice educator has concerns but the student does not, or vice versa. This again can be a useful way of beginning discussions about capability requirements. Such exercises can be used to identify areas of the student's strengths or weaknesses and can also help to clearly measure and record progress. Such evidence, if supported by clear records to underpin it, will help inform the practice educator's final recommendation and will be recorded in the final report. It will also assist those analysing final reports and recommendations particularly the Practice Assessment Panels (PAPs).

Gathering evidence – skills audit

Note: An empowering approach to the questionnaire in Figure 6.1 is to ask strengths-based questions when the student has completed the task. For example:

Case Example: The student records their ability to manage their diary as a 3

Practice educator: Great, now what are all the things that make it a 3 rather than a 1? The student may at that point be encouraged to identify areas of her diary management where she does have strengths:

Student: Well I always remember to bring my diary to meetings. I do record appointments.

Practice educator: That sounds very effective so why do you still identify your ability in this areas as a 3? What would make it a 4?

Date	1 Assessment of student's capabilities in relation to skills or knowledge Student – Yanto Smith Practice educator – Grace Briggs	1 2 3 4 5 6 7 8 9 10 1 = weak, 10 = strong 1 (Student's assessment followed by practice educator assessment)	Tasks for completion To improve skills or knowledge base	Target date for improvement and review
11.12.14	Managing my diary	Student: 1 1 2 3 4 5 6 7 8 9 10 Practice educator: 1 2 3 4 5 6 7 8 9 10	Book and attend admin. Work-shop on using electronic diary Leave travel time Update practice educator and discuss in supervision	02.2.15
15.1.15	Completing written records such as case records correctly	Student: 1 1 2 3 4 5 6 7 8 9 10 Practice educator: 1 1 2 3 4 5 6 7 8 9 10	Book and attend training course on 20.1.15 Review university notes on record keeping and feedback form academic marked work Send case notes to manager weekly for formative feedback	15.3.15
15.1.15	Knowledge of mental health legislation	Student: 1 1 2 3 4 5 6 7 8 9 10 Practice educator: 1 1 2 3 4 5 6 7 8 9 10	Review lecture notes Choose and discuss one case and related legislation in each supervision session	30.3.15

Figure 6.1 Skills Audit for Yanto Smith

Table 6.1   Skills audit template

Assessment of student's confidence in identified skills or tasks Student: _____ Practice educator: _____	Scale 1 2 3 4 5 6 7 8 9 10 Not confident Confident (students assessment followed by practice educator assessment)
1 Skill or Task 1:	Student 1 2 3 4 5 6 7 8 9 10 Practice educator 1 2 3 4 5 6 7 8 9 10 (Date agreed: review progress _____)
2 Skill or Task 2:	Student 1 2 3 4 5 6 7 8 9 10 Practice educator 1 2 3 4 5 6 7 8 9 10 (Date agreed: review progress _____)
3 Skill or Task 3:	Student 1 2 3 4 5 6 7 8 9 10 Practice educator 1 2 3 4 5 6 7 8 9 10 (Date agreed: review progress _____)

Student: I don't leave enough time for travel. I'm always late, that makes me panic and I have to leave meetings early. I sometimes miss the beginning or end of the meeting and don't get the future dates as a result of that.

The student and practice educator then have two clear targets to set for the student to demonstrate improvement:

1. Student to leave agreed amount of travel time between meetings.
2. Student to ensure she is recording all appointments in her diary by staying to the end of meetings.

The above exercise is one example of how a practice educator might assess and gather evidence of progress, to support their midway report and final recommendation. How the practice educator will gather evidence is usually discussed at the placement agreement meeting but evidence will be gathered in a variety of ways throughout placement.

It is important to remind ourselves at this stage that while problems or difficulties might be owned by the student, equally such issues may emanate with the placement or practice educator. A willingness to openly and honestly identify and address such issues is paramount to providing an effective learning environment. The student should always have had access to all the agencies policies and procedures including those associated with supervision, bullying in the workplace and whistle-blowing procedure. (A copy of the HEI whistle-blowing policy can usually be found in the student handbook. The complaints procedure is also available in this handbook and the student should be encouraged to read this before starting the placement.) The skills audit template (Table 6.1) is provided here for use in this context and the example of a completed audit is also provided.

Working with others

In taking on a student, practice educators have agreed to be responsibile for making the final recommendation. This decision can ultimately be called into question by moderation panels. However, triangulating our evidence and following the guidance in Chapters 3 and 4 will help to make your recommendation and report robust. Practice educators should also secure feedback from work-based supervisors (if applicable) and colleagues. In the main, teams tend to be helpful, working openly to promote a student's development, and provide clear honest feedback. However, on some occasions teams, for the kindest of reasons, minimize the issues a student might have been ignoring, are unmet or persistent practice issues. On the other hand individuals or wider placement teams may transfer their own issues on to the student, raising concerns about students practice with no clear evidence to underpin their comments.

Sometimes, particularly with final-year students, the placement team can begin to see a competent student as a fully-fledged social worker and expect the student to manage caseloads and responsibilities equal to those of a qualified, paid, member of staff. Some students may be flattered by this but always remember that students should be *supernumerary* to staffing numbers.

It is possible, particularly within teams where there have been recent or ongoing difficulties such as redundancies or investigations, that underlying tensions can impact negatively on students. There can be pressure for teams who have always taken student placements to keep offering such opportunities, with no consideration of changes in circumstances. Students cannot, and should not, be overly sheltered from the reality of the pressures within social work settings as much can be learnt from such situations, but where a safe learning environment cannot be offered we urge those being approached to provide student placement to inform the HEI of any significant change in circumstances.

Practice educator and student relationship

The **placement agreement meeting** is the setting to clarify and establish everyone's roles. How the student will be assessed and given feedback about their ability to meet the requirements of the course will be fully discussed. The relationship between student and practice educator is critical and having an awareness of your own personality and working style is helpful. For example, if you are aware that you tend to be someone who is very risk averse this might transfer into the way you allocate work opportunities to the student rather than allocating work based on the student's assessed ability. Such a situation if not addressed could become a barrier to the student's development and cause the student to either doubt in their own abilities reducing their levels of self-efficacy or make the student feel frustrated and disillusioned with the placement. Using a model of supervision and a negotiated supervision contract can be valuable in establishing and managing expectations of roles (see Chapter 2).

Of course, students and practice educators come from a broad range of backgrounds and differences might occur across gender, ethnicity, age, disability, class or sexuality. These differences alongside the power dynamics between student and assessor should always be acknowledged. Use supervision to explore how such differences might impact on the placement experience. Again a negotiated supervision contract can be one way of recording how issues resulting from diversity can be addressed. The practice educator should continuously develop their own supervision, critically reflecting on their own values and beliefs and exploring any issues that might arise as a result in order to recognize potential for oppressive or discriminatory practice.

When problems persist, what next?

Concerns meetings

These meetings are sometimes known by other names such as progress review meetings. The main thing to remember is that they can be requested at any time during the placement and can be called by anyone involved in the process, including the student. However, it is usually the practice educator who requests the commencement of this formal process. Attendees at such meetings can vary but should always include the student (who is permitted to bring someone along with them for support, such as a friend or student union representative), the practice educator, the tutor (who in the absence of a head of course year or senior member of the team will take responsibility for chairing the meeting). These meetings are often held within the HEI. On occasions an administrator will attend to take a record of points discussed.

These meetings allow all those present to hear the concerns being raised along with the evidence that underpins them. The student will have an opportunity to offer their own opinions and evidence relating to the situation, and usually a plan is then agreed which will offer the student clear goals to aim for within an agreed timescale. All parties will need to work together to produce clear plans of how identified concerns will be addressed.

Very occasionally, placements may be immediately suspended while further evidence of potential serious problems is collated, and in exceptional circumstances placements may be terminated with no further opportunity for the student to go back to placement. Such a decision to terminate a placement would only usually take place in the event of gross misconduct/dangerous practice. In the case of a suspected breach of the HCPC code of practice, the student's professional suitability would be in question. In this instance, the HEI will instigate fitness-to-practice proceedings. This is a formal process within the HEI and, because of the seriousness of the allegations, the proceedings are strictly confidential. The student is notified and usually precluded from further practice or study while these proceedings are in progress. Fitness-to-practice investigations findings operate on a 'balance of probability' rather than 'beyond reasonable doubt' basis as the protection of service users is the primary concern. If the allegation calling into question fitness to practice is proven, then outcomes vary according to the HEI but usually include one or more of the actions below:

- The student may continue on the course with no further action taken.
- The student may be allowed to continue on the course but with conditions in place.
- A formal warning may be issued and kept on record.
- The placement may be terminated. Alternative placement may or may not be recommended.
- The student may be required to leave the course because they have been found unfit to practice.
- A report may be made to the relevant professional body (usually the HCPC) and the student's employer, if applicable.

Higher education institutions have clear guidelines in their handbooks and policies relating to the timescales, which need to be adhered to. Practice educators should ensure that they read the relevant HEI's policy and, if they remain unsure about their role in this process, seek guidance from a colleague in the HEI.

In the vast majority of cases, no such incidents occur and the practice educator needs to simply make the final assessment decision.

Making the final assessment decision

As already noted the practice educator has to analyse information from the assessment of a student and make the final recommendation. The options open to a practice educator will depend on the HEI but generally these will include:

Pass – the student has attained the standard required for their course level.
Fail – the student has not met the standard required for their course level.
  (Some HEIs will only offer one of the above two recommendations.)
Refer – in some HEIs, practice educators are permitted to offer this as an alternative recommendation. An example might be that a student has shown some development but has not fully met criteria for passing (usually owing to a difficulty such as ill health) and it is felt that a further placement would offer the opportunity to evidence their ability to attain the required standards.
Defer – used when a student requests a break from studies while they address personal issues, such as relationship breakdown or bereavement.

Managing a failed or referred placement

Making a recommendation of a fail or refer for a student on placement can be an extremely stressful time for a practice educator and for the wider team. This should be acknowledged and managed through the support systems identified and discussed in Chapter 7. There can be an overwhelming awareness of the fact that failing a student could lead to the end of their aspirations to become a social worker (although students can appeal against the recommendation). It is important to remember that while much emphasis is put on the professional judgement of the practice educator, and much store set by it, your recommendation is still just that – a recommendation. As well as encouraging best placement practice and opportunities, the QAPL process, to some extent protects the student from unsubstantiated decisions on part of a practice educator, and the PEP and course assessment board will make the final decisions.

There may be a real sense of failure or anxiety if the student and or the HEI do not agree with the practice educator's recommendation, and the practice educator may wish to explore such issues with someone from the HEI. Once the placement has reached this formal stage, work undertaken by the practice educator such as evidence of clear assessments, formative feedback, defined appropriate learning opportunities, colleague feedback and supervision notes will prove invaluable. Well-recorded, accessible evidence will assist the QAPL process to go smoothly and will evidence how the practice educator has reached their final recommendation.

As with all work undertaken within the social work field it is important that we all seek and secure the best 'good' outcome possible even if the outcome is not one we had wished for. Working with a failing student can of course be difficult, but managing a good ending provides a level of dignity, hope and reassurance to students and practice educators, as well as being a valuable practical step to the next stage of the student's career.

Off-site practice educators who work on a freelance basis tend to work in much greater isolation than their on-site colleagues and may find that they have less opportunity for informal peer supervision. In such situations it is imperative that the off-site practice educator utilizes their own supervision as well as linking with the HEI tutor in order to evaluate the placement process.

Once it has been agreed that a placement should be terminated a notice of termination form is completed (usually by the tutor) and this will be presented along with the practice educator's final report to the PEP. Writing a final report for a student who might have been on placement only for a few weeks or whom you have found it very difficult to support can be a daunting task. Although there will inevitably be gaps, the format will remain the same as for any final report. This document is extremely important. In addition to helping to provide evidence to the moderation panel about the issues identified and the support given, it will offer the student a clear account of where their work fell below the required standards. Practice educators should not be afraid they will dilute their concerns about a student's ability by identifying areas where the student showed strengths or potential. As has already been noted, such feedback might assist the student in finding a more appropriate course or career. Alternatively, if the PEP feels that the student should be offered a further opportunity of placement then the report will offer clearly the situation to the next practice educator and allow them to plan for the next placement opportunity.

Duffy (2003) examined practice educators reluctance to fail students. The following points were among the reasons:

- Feeling that it is too late in the placement (and concerns were not raised early enough or evidence was not gathered to support concerns).
- Lack of confidence about their own professional judgement as practice educators.
- Concerns about the impact on a potential fail on the student's personal life; for example, they may have children to support.
- Avoidance of stress and discomfort on the part of the practice educator.
- Being unclear about what constitutes 'good enough' practice.

Note: On the point of good enough practice; it is useful to remember the criterion-referenced approach. You should be taking and measuring students against the levels of progression stipulated for the PCF at the end of each student placement and note that may differ from expectations of capability of employed staff. For further reading in this area, Thompson (2006) offers a tool to aid assessment with 'borderline' passing or failing students.

Practice educators who find themselves struggling to recommend a fail although they feel strongly it is the right assessment, ought to gain confidence from considering objectively whether their assessment is criterion referenced and well evidenced (see Chapter 3) as well as considering if they are being unduly effected by any of the points above. The National Organization for Practice Teaching (NOPT 2013) offers further guidance on dealing with failing placements in its *Code of Practice for Practice Educators*. It is important to remember that to shirk the responsibility to recommend a fail for a student who is not able to meet the criteria does no one any favours. You lose credibility with other professionals who quickly realize your assessment was flawed. The students, should they be allowed to progress, or worse, qualify, find they are either unable to secure employment or very quickly encounter problems when they do start practising, but most of all, service users are not protected from poor or inadequate practice.

Wider support services

Empathy, flexibility, and creativity are all valued in the practice educator role but clear expectations and boundaries are also there to protect the practice educator–student relationship. The focus must be maintained on delivering a quality learning experience. The role of practice educator does not include best friend relationship or debt counsellor or therapist. Practice educators are not responsible, for example, for assisting a student to secure and pass an assignment they should have completed prior to placement. What a practice educator will need to know is how and where a student might access appropriate support to address such issues. The HEI often provides direct access to such services and the practice educator should refer the student to their tutor or to student services to access them.

Practical Tips: Quick guide to where students might secure additional support if they face problems while on placement

- ☑ HEI tutor
- ☑ HEI course leader
- ☑ HEI placement coordinator
- ☑ Student learning support
- ☑ Student Union
- ☑ Peers, friends or family
- ☑ Specific support groups within HEI, for example, finance, housing, disability, black and ethnic minority, gay, lesbian, bisexual student support
- ☑ Citizens Advice Bureau (for issues such as housing money/debt advice or relationship breakdown)
- ☑ General practitioner or practice nurse (for physical or mental health issues).

Tackling your student's learning needs

Case Example: Identifying opportunities that indicate a student's needs

Jan was a second-year student on her first social work placement with a voluntary sector agency which supported young care leavers. Jan had previously worked as a youth support worker for six years and in the main her work had involved taking young carers on short breaks. Prior to this Jan had undertaken a host of service industry jobs which she had alongside caring for a close family member who died a few years ago. Claire had access to Jan's PAF prior to the informal interview and had noted that Jan felt her skills were all 'very practical'. Later at the informal interview Jan had talked about her past experience with young people and had shared her hopes of 'getting back into real work with young people and away from the demands of academic pieces of work which she didn't really enjoy'. Claire was impressed by Jan's keenness to work with young people and identified many transferable skills Jan would bring with her to the team.

The placement agreement meeting was rushed, with all parties keen to complete and move on to other meetings, but when asked by the tutor about learning opportunities Claire mentioned the case notes and review reports which Jan would be expected to complete as part of her role. Jan made a comment about 'paper work getting in the way of real work' but this did not get any response and was not recorded. The practice educator had observed Jan settle into the team well and appeared to be enjoying meeting service users and shadowing colleagues on home visits to see the young people. However, Claire became increasingly conscious that Jan appeared to struggle with both her organizational skills and with any written tasks. In supervision Jan usually gave a plausible reason why she had not completed such written tasks. Colleagues from reception had been overheard discussing how the student never appeared to get back to other professionals who were leaving messages.

Jan went off sick in her seventh week on placement and during the first couple of days of Jan's absence a service user had approached the team asking if Jan had completed the letter she had promised him weeks ago. The service user noted the deadline for him to access a course he had applied for was that day and he needed to pass on this letter with his application form. Claire looked in the files for this letter but eventually found it started but unfinished in Jan's desk.

In reading through the above Case Example you might find it easy to identify where this student might have been challenged about her motivation in relation to written tasks in social work practice and supported to improve her skills. Very early opportunities to challenge the student's prioritization and valuing of 'very practical skills' at the expense of academic and recording skills were blatantly missed. The opportunity to test out concerns by entering into open and honest dialogue with the student was not taken up by the practice educator during supervision. A further opportunity to arrange to observe the student undertaking a written piece of work was missed as was requesting formal feedback from colleagues who had been overheard discussing issues relating to the students work. The practice educator could have also used self-assessment exercises in supervision to ascertain the student's own perception of her ability to complete written tasks. Once a learning need had been clearly identified the practice educator and student would have been able to plan some clear goals, such as completing a formal

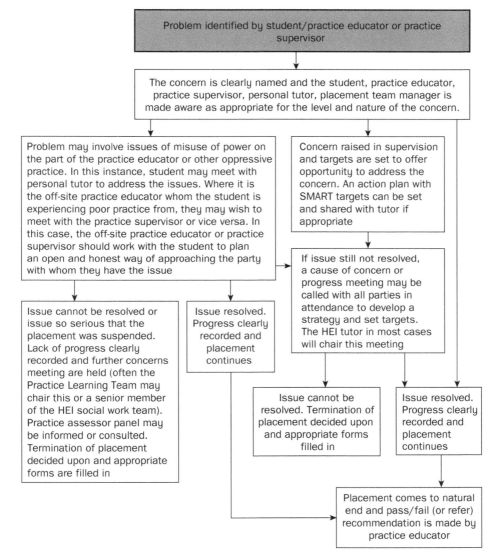

Figure 6.2 Addressing Problems and Concerns on Placement

letter to a good standard in a set time frame or writing up team-meeting minutes, again within an agreed time frame. As professionals we are used to appropriately challenging individuals. Our work with students should be no different, developing a mutual agreement of how each party might appropriately challenge an issue in supervision can make such situations easier to address.

The flow chart (Figure 6.2) shows the process we would recommend for addressing persistent problems of concern relating to a student's practice on a placement. Details can usually be found in the student handbook or are available through the HEI.

7 Final thoughts – your own personal and professional development

Introduction

As has been discussed, practice educators are now required to achieve the practice educator awards at either level 1 or 2. These awards build competence in PEPS and adherence to social work values as they apply to practice education. Throughout this book, we have indicated where your work will link to those standards. Whether you have qualified, intend to qualify or are content being a work-based supervisor, use the PEPS as your compass to keep you on course and as a basis for your own reflective practice. In addition, we offer the following advice.

Looking after yourself

Practice educating students can be immensely rewarding and we have learned as much from them as they ever have from us. That is not to say that their trials and tribulations, and the nature of the work they undertake, has no impact. It is only right then to acknowledge the sometimes-emotional impact of taking a student. Ensure you use your own supervision and other formal and informal support networks to build and maintain your own resilience:

- A good practice educator will be a reflective practice educator, who regularly assesses their own practice and critically evaluates it, ensuring they adhere to the values and ethics of their profession, and that can be personally challenging!
- Taking a student is not an 'add on' to your work. It is a function that will take time and energy. It is essential then that you are able to adjust your workload accordingly.
- Stay motivated! The satisfaction of using your practice education skills to develop your skills and knowledge base can promote a strong sense of professional accomplishment and increased confidence. Where possible, undertake this as a part of an accredited or recognized CPD activity such as a practice educator award.

Use of formal and informal support systems

If you do decide to embark on the practice educator awards, you will find you have a ready-made form of support in your tutors who will often be supervising your practice and assessing your portfolios, giving formative feedback and guidance. If your place of work has supported and funded your learning, you may well also be able to access support in supervision (see below). Most courses will have built-in opportunities for sharing practice and time for discussing difficulties and challenges informally with fellow students, and many courses run practice educator support groups which welcome practice educators whether or not they are undertaking the award. In addition, many workplaces that take students have practice educator groups designed specifically to allow practice educators to provide mutual support and share resources. If your organization has many practice teachers but no practice group, why not start one?

If you are not undertaking a formal practice educator award or if you are an independent social worker, you may feel isolated. It is important to have a forum to take your practice issues to, and there are numerous options. Most universities run practice educator groups and offer supplementary training for practice educators who support their students, regardless of whether they do the practice educator award with them. Remember, you are a valuable commodity and it is in their interest to build a relationship of mutual benefit.

In today's world of social networking, most practitioners are aware of how to maintain confidentiality and ensure ethical practice online. With that in mind, most professional social work and education organizations now have blogs, Twitter addresses and, often, Facebook profiles. They can be a valuable source of current information and breaking news, especially with regard to policy development. Online discussions groups via such mediums can be a helpful way to access informal support; I have spent many happy times meeting people at conferences who I have only ever had previous contact with on Twitter or via an online discussion thread on TCSW or British Association of Social Workers (BASW) member areas, and many a useful collaboration has come of it.

Supervision

As discussed in Chapter 3, high-quality supervision for your student is of the upmost importance and you will have spent time and effort ensuring your student understands and fully participates in this professional requirement. Of course, the same goes for you.

Practical Tips: Checklist for your own supervision

- ☑ Put your practice educator work on the agenda.
- ☑ Discuss suitable work/caseload allocation for your student.
- ☑ Ask for accredited learning/practice educator training or time for practice educator group support.
- ☑ Time management relating to extra responsibility.
- ☑ Make time for reflection on your practice.

As previously discussed, supporting a social work student requires specific skills and knowledge and can on occasion prove to be both stressful and confusing, therefore your access to quality regular supervision is imperative. As part of the preparations you will need to ensure your supervisor is aware that you are taking on additional responsibility of the role of practice educator or work-based supervisor. Supervision time needs to be scheduled so your supervision needs and practice education do not get lost in dialogue relating to your wider role in the workplace, such as casework discussions. Make sure your work with your student is recorded and discussed regularly in terms of your learning and skills development and, where possible, ensure your annual performance review (APR) reflects your development and added responsibility.

Remember we cannot model good practice to students if we do not prioritize our own self-care and resilience.

Appendices

Appendix 1
PEPS Standards and values

The following standards are updated regularly and as a dynamic and changing set of standard we therefore felt it would be advisable to provide links to the appropriate standards rather than reproducing them here.

   These may be obtained from

The College of Social Work
30 Euston Square
London
NW1 2FB
Tel: 020 8436 2929
or via the following link:

http://www.tcsw.org.uk/uploadedFiles/TheCollege/_CollegeLibrary/Reform_resources/
Practice-EducatorProfessional(edref11).pdf

Appendix 2
Standards of proficiency for social workers in England

These may be obtained from

The Health and Care Professionals Council
184 Kennington Park Road
London
SE11 4BU
0845 300 6184
or via the following link:

http://www.hpc-uk.org/assets/documents/10003b08standardsofproficiency-social
workersinengland.pdf

Appendix 3
Professional capabilities framework (for end of placement 1 and 2)

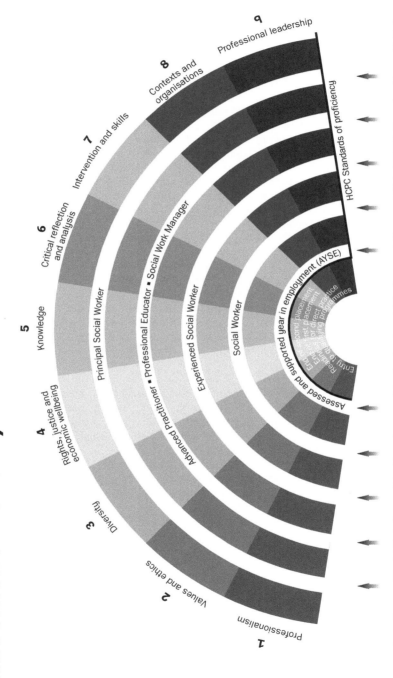

1. Professionalism
2. Values and ethics
3. Diversity
4. Rights, justice and economic wellbeing
5. Knowledge
6. Critical reflection and analysis
7. Intervention and skills
8. Contexts and organisations
9. Professional leadership

Principal Social Worker
Advanced Practitioner • Professional Educator • Social Work Manager
Experienced Social Worker
Social Worker
Assessed and supported year in employment (AYSE)
End of last placement
End of first placement
Readiness for direct practice
Entry to qualifying programmes

HCPC Standards of proficiency

References

Brown, A. and Bourne, I. (1996) *The Social Work Supervisor*. Buckingham: Open University Press.

Clifford, D.J. (1995) Methods in oral history and social work, *Journal of the Oral History Society*, 23(2): 65–70.

Croisedale-Appleby, D. (2014) *Re-Visioning Social Work Education: An Independent Review*. London: Department of Health.

Darling, L. (1986) What to do about toxic mentors, *Nurse Educator*, 11(2): 29–30.

Department for Children, Schools and Families (DCSF) (2009) *The Protection of Children in England: A Progress Report*. London: DCSF.

Dominelli, L. (2002) *Anti-oppressive social work theory and practice*. Basingstoke: Palgrave Macmillan.

Duffy, K. (2003) Failing students: a qualitative study of the factors that influence the decisions regarding assessment of students' competence in practice. Available at: http://www.nmc-uk.org/documents/Archived%20Publications/1Research%20papers/Kathleen_Duffy_Failing_Students2003.pdf [accessed 4 Sep. 2014].

Earl, L. (2004) *Assessment as Learning*, Thousand Oaks, CA: Corwin Press.

Finlay, L. (2008) Reflecting on 'reflective practice', Practice-Based Professional Learning Centre. Available at http://www.open.ac.uk/cetl-workspace/cetlcontent/documents/4bf2b48887459.pdf [accessed 27 Dec. 2012].

Fook, J. and Gardner, F. (2007) *Practising Critical Reflection*. Maidenhead: Open University Press.

Ford, K. and Jones, A. (1987) *Student Supervision*. Basingstoke: Macmillan Education.

Furness, S. and Gilligan, P. (2010) *Religion, Belief and Social Work*. Bristol: Policy Press.

Gothard, W. (2001) *Careers Guidance in Context*). London: Sage.

Honey, P. and Mumford, A. (1982) *Manual of Learning Styles*. London: P. Honey.

Howe, K. and Gray, I. (2013) *Effective supervision in social work*. Los Angeles, CA: London: Sage/Learning Matters.

Kadushin, A. (1992) *Supervision in Social Work*. New York: Columbia University Press.

Knowles, M. (1990) *The Adult Learner*. Houston, TX: Gulf.

Kurfiss, J. (1989) Helping faculty foster students' critical thinking in the disciplines, *New Directions for Teaching and Learning*, 37(Spring): 41–50.

Maslow, A. (1970) *Motivation and Personality*. New York: Harper & Row.

Morrison, T. and Wonnacott, J. (2010) Supervision: now or never. Reclaiming reflective supervision in social work, February, In-Trac Training and Consultancy. Available at http://www.in-trac.co.uk/supervision-now-or-never [accessed 27 Mar. 2014].

Munro, E. (2011) The Munro review of child protection: final report – a child-centred system. Available at: www.education.gov.uk/munroreview/downloads/8875_DFE_MunroReport_Tagged.pdf [accessed 8 Oct. 2014].

National Organization for Practice Teaching (NOPT) (2013) *Code of Practice for Practice Educators*. Accessed at: http://www.nopt.org/college-of-social-work-consultation/ [accessed 6 Oct. 2014].

Parker, J. (2004) *Effective Practice Learning in Social Work*. Exeter: Learning Matters.

Senge, P. (1990) *The Fifth Discipline*. New York: Doubleday/Currency.

Shardlow, S. and Doel, M. (1996) *Practice Learning and Teaching*. Basingstoke: Macmillan.

Taylor, C. and White, S. (2000) *Practising Reflexivity in Health and Welfare*. Buckingham: Open University.

Tennant, M. (1997) *Psychology and Adult Learning*. 2nd edn. London: Routledge.

Thompson, N. (2006) *Promoting Workplace Learning*. Bristol: Policy Press.

Thompson, N. (2009) *Promoting Equality, Valuing Diversity*. Lyme Regis: Russell House.

Walsh, D. (2010) *The Nurse Mentor's Handbook*. Maidenhead: Open University Press.

The College of Social Work (TCSW) (2012) Professional Capability Framework – End of First Placement Level Capabilities. Available at: http://www.tcsw.org.uk/uploaded-Files/PCFNOVEndofFirstPlacementCapabilities.pdf [accessed 29 Aug. 2014].

The College of Social Work (TCSW) (2014) Understanding the PCF. Available at http://www.tcsw.org.uk/pcf [accessed 29 Aug. 2014].

Index

THE SOCIAL WORK PORTFOLIO
A STUDENT'S GUIDE TO EVIDENCING YOUR PRACTICE

Lee-Ann Fenge, Kate Howe, Mel Hughes and Gill Thomas

June 2014 114pp
978-0-335-24531-4 – Paperback

eBook also available

The portfolio is an essential part of the summative assessment within qualifying social work programmes. All students are required to complete a practice portfolio to provide evidence of their learning in practice. This essential book demonstrates how students can use the portfolio to demonstrate their learning in terms of developing core knowledge, values and skills.

Topics covered include:

- What a portfolio is, and how to make best use of it in your learning journey
- How to evidence your capability using the Professional Capabilities Framework for Social Workers
- How to reflect on your own learning needs and learning style
- How to work with your practice educator in terms of practice learning and portfolio development
- How to evidence the use of theory in your portfolio
- How to evidence meaningful service user and carer involvement within your placement and portfolio
- How to use your portfolio as a basis for future CPD learning, including the need to develop Personal Development Plans and the role of AYSE

Written by a team of experts from Bournemouth University, each chapter uses a range of reflective activities, practice educator comments, and student testimony to illustrate the discussion.

www.openup.co.uk

OPEN UNIVERSITY PRESS
McGraw - Hill Education

AN INTRODUCTION TO APPLYING SOCIAL WORK THEORIES AND METHODS

Second Edition

Barbra Teater

9780335247639 (Paperback)
April 2014

eBook also available

This bestselling book is the leading introduction to the most commonly used theories and methods in social work practice. Now in its second edition, the book explores the concepts of a 'theory' and a 'method', the difference between the two and the ways in which they are connected. Assuming little to no prior knowledge, each chapter explores a single theory or method in depth and uses a variety of interactive tools to encourage the reader to explore their own theories and beliefs.

Key features:

- New chapter on **Community Work** provides a step-by-step approach to community work
- New chapter on **Groupwork** provides an overview of the rationale for groupwork
- New **case studies** exploring areas of growing priority in practice such as dementia

www.openup.co.uk

CONTEMPORARY SOCIAL WORK PRACTICE
A Handbook for Students

Barbra Teater

9780335246038 (Paperback)
February 2014

eBook also available

This exciting new book provides an overview of fifteen different contemporary social work practice settings, spanning across the statutory, voluntary, private and third sectors. It serves as the perfect introduction to the various roles social workers can have and the numerous places they can work, equipping students with the knowledge, skills and values required to work in areas ranging from mental health to fostering and adoption, and from alcohol and drug treatment services to youth offending.

Key features:

- An overview of the setting, including the role of the social worker, how service users gain access to the service and key issues, definitions or terms specific to the setting
- Legislation and policy guidance related to the specific setting
- The key theories and methods related to the setting

www.openup.co.uk